LAND on my right

A sail round Britain single-handed on a Laser, unsupported

By Ron Pattenden

Contents

1. Introduction
2. Eastbourne to Fortuneswell
3. Fortuneswell to Goran Haven
4. Goran Haven to Port Isaac
5. Port Isaac to Little Haven
6. Little Haven to Wallasey
7. Wallasey to Port Logan
8. Port Logan to Loch Stornaway
9. Loch Stornaway to Isle of Skye
10. Isle of Skye to Durness
11. Durness to Lybster
12. Lybster to Aberdeen
13. Aberdeen to St. Monans
14. St. Monans to Seahouses
15. Seahouses to Filey
16. Filey to Cromer
17. Cromer to London
18. London to Dover
19. Dover to Samphire Hoe
20. Samphire Hoe to Dymchurch
21. Dymchurch to Eastbourne

CHAPTER 1

INTRODUCTION

I first started sailing at the age of 16, when my brother and I went on a week's trip in a 30 foot Gaff rigged yacht on the Norfolk Broads.
Since then I have been on the Broads many times, mainly on the old traditional gaffers. A lot of people call it ditch crawling, and ask why I don't do some proper sea sailing.
I have been on some sea voyages, notably around the Canaries in a Benneteau, but I have to say I found them boring in that mile after mile you are on the same course, watching the instruments as there is nothing else to see. Tacking is done at a leisurely pace, since you can do it at any time.
I was also a crew member on the Hoya 60 when Linford Christie filmed his Record Breakers attempt at the fastest time for a monohull in the Round the Isle of Wight Race. This was much more interesting, but I was only cannon fodder really - just a winch man amongst a crew of 17. I still think that trying to sail a 30 foot up an 80ft wide river on the Norfolk Broads is pretty skilful, quite hairy at times and never boring apart from in the lightest of winds.
I wanted to get into sailing after my first Broads experience, but big boat sailing was too costly. However, after a particularly good week on the Broads with a Motorcycle Club mate, Chris, we decided to go halves on a Mirror Dinghy. This was a good introduction to dinghy sailing and I would recommend a Mirror to anyone starting Dinghy sailing, on a tight budget. We played around with the Mirror for a year or so at Gillingham Strand, but I couldn't always go on the days when Chris could and vice versa. I had moved to Sevenoaks from London by this time and had my name down at a new reservoir club without as yet any water - Bewl Bridge. I watched this develop into a good club and in 1977 bought my first Laser. Although I raced there occasionally, I was never a very good racer as I could never devote enough time to it.
I suppose I was, and still am, a "jack of all trades and master of none". I loved my motorcycling, both on the road and trials riding. I tried hang gliding, road and off-road cycling, walking, skiing, and squash.
In 1980 I snapped my left Achilles tendon playing squash and was told that as I was over 30 I should give up squash. This was like a red rag to a bull, and I was determined to return to squash as soon as my "sewn back" Achilles was mended. The physiotherapist said that walking and gentle jogging was the best way to get back to a reasonable level of fitness.
Within a year I entered my first marathon, and was soon back playing

squash, although I never really got back to the same standard. My left calf muscle never grew back to its original size and is still only two thirds of the size of my right one.

I sold my original old Laser and bought a brand new one. I did a winter series at Bough Beech Reservoir, but decided it was too damned cold for me. On one memorable occasion, I capsized, and as I righted her, ice was forming on the deck, and I kept sliding about until inevitably I capsized again. This time it was straight into the shore, run up to the clubhouse for a hot shower, and worry about de-rigging later. (No dry suits in those days).

I sold this Laser after a while, and bought a Contender, which is again a single-hander, but this time with a trapeze. Now this really was a challenge, especially on Bewl Reservoir with all the different wind shifts. It was great to start with being in the general handicap fleet, as I nearly always came across the finishing line first, but on corrected time all the Optimists, Mirrors etc. beat me by a mile. It got to the stage where I would shower and slope off home before the results were put up on the notice board. I also missed the close competition that one class sailing entails and as mine was the only Contender at the club, I wasn't learning anything. It was also a fag with such a large boat to de-rig and trailer it to the coast on the odd occasion. Money was a bit tight at this stage so I decided to sell the Contender and bought a really old Laser number 7670, which I believe was built in 1973. The extra money I received in the transaction probably went on food or some other frivolous item like paying the mortgage! I used to sail with my friend Guy at Bewl, but as we were sailing there less often, we didn't renew our membership and kept both boats in my garden. Over the years various bits on mine either got broken or fell apart, so I borrowed his.

By 1999, there was virtually only the hull left intact so I decided to buy another one number 46218 called Oops. Guy's Laser was then sold to Nick who often sailed with me when I went to Poole Harbour in my shiny "new" Oops.

For the odd half day's sailing I go to Cooden as it is easy to launch and close to home, but for a few days' sailing Poole is my favourite place. There is virtually no tide, and when it blows a hooley, (Sorry Hooley – Hilary's niece, Lisa, has a chocolate brown Labrador of this name) there is no swell and a broad reach on a Laser is unbeatable. Also as it is virtually land-locked, there is no real danger, therefore Hilary (my partner) and Tina (our Jack Russell) were happy to come along for picnics in different parts of the harbour. We also went to Brownsea Island, but we were told off for bringing a dog ashore which apparently is not allowed. Occasionally we went out past the chain link ferry to Studland Bay. We had some great times - it's funny how we look back through rose coloured glasses. As Mark Twain once said "I find that the further I go back, the better things were, whether they happened or not".

By 1999 I was really getting fed up with working in London, The journey was horrendous and I would leave each morning at 6.00am, and return home at 8.30pm, shattered. At this time rumours of a take-over was rife, and I was looking forward to redundancy, especially as the atmosphere in the office was so depressing. As someone said "The layoffs will continue until morale improves".

I read a book about this time called "The Sea on our Left" by Shally Hunt. It described how she walked with Richard, her husband, round the coast of Britain in ten months. I got the impression that a large part of their trip was a bit boring, especially when there was mile after mile of flat countryside on the right and the sea on the left. Poor Shally struggled every day to keep up with Richard and I also thought that starting on 1st January was a bit masochistic, knowing the British weather. It did, however, inspire me enough to think up a cunning plan to cycle round Britain. With this project in mind, I knew it would take much less time, maybe four or five months, but I wouldn't be able to do it unless I gave up work.

I eventually took early retirement at the age of fifty one, in June 2001. Hilary also retired at this time and we decided that with a reduced income all holidays from now on would have to be SKI ones (Spending the Kid's Inheritance). That year we had a great time camping along with the bears in the Canadian Rockies, and in our campervan round Ireland. I was, however, planning our cycling trip for 2002.

In 1999 we bought a tandem, as we were always going at different speeds to each other on our ordinary bikes, we decided that this was a better way of staying together.

By the beginning of May 2002 I had everything prepared, and we set off with all our worldly goods, (including Tina in a basket in front) round Britain. We covered 4700 miles in 4 months, following the coast, as near as possible, by road. As we had to carry everything with us we soon worked out what we really needed and what to leave behind. We camped every night apart from one when Pete, who we met in Polperro with a group of cyclists, put us up when we reached his house in Portishead.

We had some pretty awful weather that year and our idea of stopping for a few days here and there on some wonderful beaches never came to fruition. Instead we just kept pushing on and parts of the trip became a bit of a chore, trying to get to a camp site before the big black cloud ahead had a chance to dump its load on us. Although campsites are fairly plentiful along the coast, they always seem to appear earlier in the day than we intended to stop, so we often camped rough. This was fine as long as we could take a shower every other day, and in fact we prefer camping rough. You go camping to get away from it all and on most sites you usually end up two feet away from the next tent, especially in the high season.

Having completed this challenge, 2003 seemed to be getting boring to me, as we had no real aim after skiing, apart from touring round Cornwall in the summer in our campervan. We planned a two month trip around the world with Hilary's sister and partner Margaret and Tim for the beginning of 2004, taking in California, Fiji, six weeks in a campervan round the north and south islands of New Zealand, then back via Australia and Singapore. It was during this trip that my next cunning plan was formed - Round Britain on a Laser. I had often thought about a trip like this, but I had always scared myself out of it. This time however, once the seed had been sown, I couldn't stop thinking about it, and convinced myself that there were various "get - out clauses". I intended to hug the coast so at any time if things got too hairy for me I could beach the boat - a quick phone call home and that's it - challenge over.

I realised it wasn't quite as simple as that since there are stretches even in the relatively benign areas of the south coast where the cliffs come right down to the sea, and it could be miles before a beaching operation could be put into practice. In such areas, I would always make sure that the weather was reasonable and I had plenty of daylight left before attempting to sail past.

This led me to think about what to do if the wind died completely. A canoe paddle was the only answer, as I thought an outboard motor would be cheating, and would take up too much room, - what would happen to it in a capsize? Even on the first day I would have to go round Beachy Head, and the Seven Sisters, before a proper landing could be executed.

I had long discussions with Hilary who realised that after last year's relatively "easy" summer I needed a challenge, and she could see my enthusiasm had transformed me from a "the bottle's half empty" person to a "the bottle's half full" one. The first step to getting the things you want out of life is this: decide what you want. I said I didn't want her to support me, as it would be difficult keeping in contact, and I would worry about her being on her own especially if I was stuck at sea late in the evening.

It was also quite likely that I would land often on isolated beaches, where she couldn't drive to. With a tent and emergency food, I could just camp next to Oops, or nearby, as long as there is a flattish area above high tide level. She did make me promise, however, that I would always phone or text every night to make sure I was safe before it got dark. This was a sensible precaution, but I didn't realise how many miles I would have to leg it in the coming months to either get a signal on the mobile, or to get to a phone box. When we got back from our world tour I started preparing for my trip. The biggest problem was how to drag the boat up above high tide every time I beached it. Sod's law says it will nearly always be low tide when I land, and there can be some pretty inhospitable beaches around. I obviously couldn't take a trolley with me, and I couldn't just drag it up every time as this would wear the bottom away in no time. I thought the best suggestion was to use a yacht fender or two to roll it up. I was told that was how they did it at the Eastbourne Sovereign Sailing Club. After a few experiments I decided that just one fender was the answer. Simply put it under the front (bows), go round to the back (stern), lift and push like a wheelbarrow, retrieve the fender and repeat. This worked fairly well for short pulls, and was only a real problem when the tide was out on huge beaches like Blackpool where it took literally hours to push Oops up past the high tide line.

We had the opportunity of a week's skiing in Verbier, Switzerland, at Easter, so preparations were abandoned for a week, but when I came back I was really fired up and raring to go.

I wrote a letter to Yachts and Yachting asking if they would publish it in their "Readers Letters" column. It outlined what I intended doing, and asked was there anyone out there who had done anything like it before, and could give any advice, or support for me or my Charity on the way round. I did get one or two replies but most people thought it was a mad idea and even Yachts and Yachting changed the title of my article from "Round Britain on a Laser" to "Round the Twist".

My dad died four years ago of Prostate Cancer, and I decided to do the challenge for the Prostate Cancer Charity. Lesley, who works for the charity sent me a fundraising pack and a supply of 'T' shirts. She suggested that I set up a website which has been very good, and is still open if anyone would like to donate on line albeit now long after the challenge has been completed. The site is www.justgiving.com/ronsailing.

My dad probably wouldn't have approved of me doing such a dangerous challenge. I am 55 years old - too old to be sent to war, and 10 years older than Nelson when he went to Trafalgar. My dad knew war, but in common with most people of my age I have lived in relative safety. I have only had to decide what house or car to buy, where to go on holiday, which safe job to apply for. I think there are a lot of people like me for whom an adrenalin fix is needed - life is not dangerous enough, so let's go and make it so. Some unfortunately become football hooligans, but I prefer to be a bit more pro-active. My dad always said "Bring back conscription - that'll sort 'em out." I think he was right, I often regretted not being forced to join the army just for a few years, to get a taste of what war would possibly be like. In that way maybe our natural instinct for excitement can be channelled into something more productive. (Assuming you survive of course).

The next thing to do was to go over the boat with a fine tooth comb. Everything on the hull seemed sound - I wasn't worried about all the scratches, there will be plenty more of them in the months to come. I took off all fittings, replaced some, and made sure they were all sound and had solid fixings. I replaced all the rivets on the mast and boom, and where I could, I used stainless steel nuts and bolts rather than rivets.

I had 3 elderly sails, (one to use and two spares) that I thought would do for some of the voyage, although I assumed I would have to dig into the pockets and buy one or two on the way. My theory is - if it ain't broke, don't fix it, and besides I have short arms but deep pockets, in other words as tight as a duck's arse - and that's water tight. I would not be setting the sail for racing so it would be baggy and not fully stretched. This would also mean less strain on sail as well as the mast, boom, kicking strap etc. After all I would be sailing for many hours per day, and you can't sail in racing mode for more than an hour or two. When I was racing I used to be shattered after a one and a half hour race in a force four or five.

My tiny two man tent would do fine, I bought a new down filled sleeping bag, which looks huge when unfolded, but packs into a really small bag, and if you will excuse the pun is "featherweight". It weighs less than one kilo. The only problem with these bags is that if they get wet they are useless - they lose all insulating qualities. Oh well I'll just have to keep it dry then. I will need a sleeping mat and a few clothes. (Hilary insists on seven pairs of pants - mon/tues etc. whereas I prefer twelve pairs - jan/feb etc.) I will be in a wet suit most of the time so very few clothes will be needed.

I have been advised not to wear a dry suit, as it will be far too hot during the summer. A small camping-gaz cooker, billycans, KFS, the inevitable Swiss Army knife, a few spare tools, cleats, shackles, ropes etc. along with my sewing kit for the sails, a small VHF radio, and my mobile phone for emergencies. I also have my £5 pocket radio that is invaluable - it gives me the shipping forecast daily, and news, weather and entertainment when I am stuck in the tent for hours in the pouring rain. Oh, and last but not least my one luxury - a lifesaving hot water bottle.

Most of these items go into three waterproof bags and will be tied to the deck, two in front and one behind the mast. Not everything will go in the bags , as I have a small circular hatch in the hull which I have been able to put loads of empty two litre plastic lemonade bottles into, to keep it buoyant even if I get a really, really big hole in it. I have also dangled a thin rope which I can attach with quick release shackles, a few long thin bags containing the sails, spare drinking water, emergency food (tins) and mast repair kit.

Now I need to look at navigation and navigation aids. My "chart table" consists of a small piece of Perspex screwed to the deck next to the centreboard cut out. There is also a nautical compass attached. I have a GPS but how can I operate it whilst sailing? When we cycled round Britain we just used an AA four mile to the inch road map cut into fifty mile stretches. What's wrong with that I thought? I reckoned I could do an average of thirty miles per day sailing - some days sixty or seventy, some days five or ten, and some days none whilst sitting on a beach watching the big waves, when it is blowing a hooley. OK so out with my tried and tested method - a length of string seven and a half inches long, which represents thirty miles. Carefully go round the coastline marking off each day. Although I know it is six thousand miles round, I actually made it 3350 miles by cutting across small bays, and estuaries at a reasonable distance. This figure is misleading as I will often be tacking, and therefore doing more miles than planned. I also know that I will sometimes be doing five knots, but will be going nowhere against the current. On the other hand there will also be times when I will be doing five knots with no wind at all when the current is with me.

It should therefore only take four months, and I will be home before the end of summer. But will I be able to average thirty miles per day - that is the 64000 dollar question. Having marked the map I then cut it into strips making sure there was a reasonable overlap, and that points of reference were marked. They were laid out and taped onto A4 paper, front and back, then laminated onto (incredibly) only eleven sheets. This was done in true Blue Peter style - only the finest sticky backed plastic used here. These eleven sheets turned out to be all I needed, and along with my compass served me well throughout the journey. I studied and folded these maps before setting out each day, and made sure they were secure under my Perspex "chart table".

Surprisingly the scale of these maps was perfectly adequate. Sandbanks that are not marked were my only worry, although I would always speak to locals (especially fishermen) when I knew I was in a dodgy area, like Morecambe Bay, which people have told me is a nightmare.

So there I was all packed up and ready to go. Having decided that, in theory, it could be done in one hundred and twelve days, I added a twenty five per cent contingency for bad weather (twenty eight days). That makes one hundred and forty days - back by the end of September at worst. I felt I needed to be home before the weather deteriorates and gets too cold in the autumn.

Starting on 1st May, from Eastbourne Pier in a clockwise direction was my target, as that was the date and place that we started our cycle trip, two years ago. You need to set a target and try to stick to it, or else you may end up with the old saying "Never put off until tomorrow what you can avoid altogether".

Also having got through "Mayday" on the first day of the trip, I hoped it would be the only time I would have to use "Mayday" again, especially on the VHF radio.

Clockwise seemed the sensible way round, as the south west prevailing wind should be with me most of the time up the west coast from Land's End right up to Cape Wrath. This theory certainly didn't work when Guy and I cycled from Lands End to John o'Groats in 1992 - we had the wind against us most of the way.

During the last week of April, I practised rigging the boat which I tried to simplify by using quick release shackles, wherever possible. I also took it to Cooden for a "dress rehearsal" to make sure all the bags were secure even after a capsize drill. I decided that a belt and braces followed by another set of belt and braces, was the best approach. Why use one bit of string, when four would do. The weather was fairly calm so it was difficult to see if all would be well, but I was fairly confident that I could at least drag Oops easily up the beach with only one fender.

The first two days would be close to home and Hilary said she would meet me, and bring anything I had forgotten. She brought Tina with her both nights and we all camped together - just like the old days.

CHAPTER 2

EASTBOURNE TO FORTUNESWELL

All the sea based tales that you are about to read actually happened, but one or two of the shore based ones can be taken with a pinch of salt (water?). They only probably happened in my vivid imagination, but add a bit of humour that Tony Blackburn would be proud of. The art is to work out which ones really are genuine.

<u>Saturday May 1st</u>
I arrived at Pevensey Bay at 11.00. It is difficult to get near to Eastbourne Pier to launch, so two or three extra miles won't hurt. Guy, Rose, Lauren, Hilary and Tina came to see me off along with Terry, the photographer from the local newspaper. It's always difficult launching when Tina's around if she is not on a lead, as she will always try to sneak aboard at the last minute. I sailed in light winds to the "official start", where Olly and Helen also came to say goodbye. The time of 1.00 was therefore the official start. The green lights flashed on, I revved up and I was off on the great adventure!!! It seemed like a bit of an anti-climax. Sailing off in light airs didn't seem so intrepid - more like a lazy afternoon jolly. That was soon to change over the next few weeks however.
As I left, Hilary said "Try to get to Birling Gap at least, Seaford would be better, but not Exceat, as that is a good mile's walk from the car park".
I drifted gently past Eastbourne, which has some impressive Victorian and Georgian buildings. This fashionable resort dates back to 1780 when George III's children spent their summer holidays here. The weather is usually good here, as there is a sort of micro-climate whereby Beachy Head provides shelter from south west winds and breaks up the clouds, which is why Eastbourne often has more sunshine than anywhere else in the UK.
Slowly round my first big headland - Beachy Head - no problem, what's all the fuss about? The spectacular chalk cliffs at 530ft make the 142ft lighthouse at their foot look like a toy. From the top you can see from Dungeness in the east to the Isle of Wight in the west. At the base of the signal tower near Lover's Leap is carved a verse of the 93rd Psalm:
"Mightier than the thunders of many waters, mightier than the waves of the sea, the Lord on high is mighty".
Then it was on past Birling Gap, where there are only a few cottages left on the edge of the cliff. The rest have literally fallen into the sea. I then managed six of the Seven Sisters (sailed past them that is - nothing rude). The last one

was becoming tiresome as the wind dropped to nothing, so out with the paddle - it worked - and I just about managed to get to guess where - that's right Exceat by 8.00. I only managed eight miles, not a good start.
I walked to the car park to meet Hilary and Tina, then walked the mile back to Oops with her sleeping bag etc. where we camped the night. It was the right decision not to have her supporting me, as I would not want to do all this walking each night and morning.

Sunday May 2nd
We were on the Seven Sisters National Park land, and the Ranger came by at about 8.00 to tell us off for camping there. That was the first night, I wonder how many more "illegal" camp sites I will pitch my tent on?
I left at 10.00 still with virtually no wind, and at 1.00 had only managed to get past Seaford Head standing 282ft high to Seaford. At the beach's eastern end is the first of the 74 Martello towers built between Seaford and Folkstone to protect the coast from Napoleonic invasion. I watched the dinghies drift back to the sailing club at the end of their race. I was tempted to join them when a slight breeze popped up. It wasn't much but I managed to get past Newhaven, avoiding the cross channel ferries, past Peacehaven, where a monument on the cliffs marks where the Greenwich meridian - Zero Degrees longitude - leaves England. Then on past Roedean, where the massive grey and red buildings of Roedean's famous girls' school are.
I know a rugby song about Roedean, but perhaps we don't want to go there. Then it was on past Brighton, known fondly as "London by the Sea". Although not the first seaside resort, it set the pace since Prince Regent, Later George IV made it fashionable after his visit in 1783. On past Hove and the 350ft Portslade power station, the busy port of Shorehan-by-sea, the 960ft pier at Worthing and finally to Goring by 6.30.
My son Ian and his partner Liz arrived along with Hilary and Tina, so off for a slap up meal, then back to put the tent up in the car park.

Monday May 3rd
Off at about 10.00 with an emotional farewell. If all goes well I won't need Hilary support from now on, as the drive from home each day gets greater. Tina managed to sneak aboard again just as I set off so I had to land thirty seconds after launching and gave her to Hilary to hold. She's a little monkey!!! At last a decent wind force 3 to 4, but as it is a south westerly, I was still tacking most of the day.
A pretty uninspiring coastline, past Littlehampton, Felpham, then Queen Victoria's "Dear little Bognor". The name Bognor is derived from the Saxon word for a rocky shore. It was founded by Sir Richard Hotham, a London

Hatter in the 18th Century, who wanted to call it "Hothampton." The "Regis" was added in 1928 when George V recuperated here. When he was told that he was coming here he apparently said "Bugger Bognor." After Pagham harbour comes Selsey Bill, a low lying headland, where it's coast has been eroded this century more than any other part of Britain.

Once round the headland I was able to get a reasonable reach past Bracklesham, East Wittering, and almost up to Chichester harbour, when the wind died, so I had to paddle into the harbour and spied the Hayling Island Sailing Club, where I was able to get a shower, a beer, but unfortunately no food. I walked into town and got some fish and chips, then back to the club where they told me I couldn't put the tent up in their grounds, so I had to lug all my gear half a mile to the edge of a local tip. Nice !!!

Tuesday May 4th
Today is International Star Wars day - May the fourth be with you. I listened to the shipping forecast which was not good - Gale Force 8 with heavy rain. Even the Portsmouth ferries just round the corner had to be cancelled, so no chance of me sailing today.
This is only my fourth day, and already I'm two days behind my original schedule. Between showers I managed to put some filler in a couple of suspect cracks in the hull. I had developed a slight leak yesterday, and hope this would sort it out. So I spent another night on the exclusive Hayling Island rubbish tip.

Wednesday May 5th
I listen to the shipping forecast at 5.45 each day. Today in this area it is a south westerly force 4 to 5. As usual Rockall are having nothing!!! I started at 7.00 in very confused seas. There is still a large swell following yesterday's gales. I had to go quite a long way out to sea to get round the sandbank just off Eastoke Point. The tide and wind are against me so I am making very little headway. I can feel that the hull is filling up with sea water so I stop every hour or so to empty out.
I went past Eastney, Southsea, and missed Portsmouth, where HMS Victory is in Dry Dock. This is the famous ship in which Nelson died in 1805 during the Battle of Trafalgar. I don't know if Hardy ever did kiss Nelson on his death bed, or anywhere else for that matter. The Victory is still the flagship of the Commander-in-Chief Naval Home Command. I sailed past Spithead, where Fleet Reviews are carried out.
By 3.30 just past Stokes Bay, I noticed a small tear in the sail so I decided to give up for the day, and pulled Oops up onto an isolated beach near Lee-on-the-Solent, having done only ten miles in eight hours.

An Army Land Rover came to tell me I was on MOD land, but after I explained that I was sailing round Britain for the Prostate Cancer Charity, he said it was OK for me to camp there and showed me a short cut to the nearest pub - good man.

I sorted the sail out - a stitch in time, and all that. Then I set about fixing the hull. There were no obvious holes which led me to think it must be a leak where the mast is stepped. I filled it up with water and watched the level drop immediately - so that's the problem then. I cut a piece of wood, (with my Swiss Army knife - in true boy scout fashion) and popped it in the hole covered in gooey filler, then rammed it home with the handle end of the paddle. There's not much more I can do till I do some "Sea-Trials" tomorrow, so it's off to the pub, now fully clothed in wet weather gear, as it's now pouring with rain. My friend, Guy's motto has always been "Your legacy should be that you make it better than it was before". It doesn't always work in his case though.

Thursday May 6th
I woke early to listen to the forecast - south westerly (again) force 3 to 4. I started at 7.00 and on the second tack, I was heading for Cowes on the Isle of Wight. I decided to land at Cowes a) to empty out the hull which is still leaking, and b) just to say I've sailed across to the Island and I didn't have to pay for a ferry.

Cowes is one of the most fashionable yachting centres in the world. The Royal Yacht Squadron, founded in 1815, is reckoned to be the most exclusive yacht club in the world. It's a greystone building, with battlements and a semi-circle of 22 brass cannons which was adapted from a 16th century fort built by Henry VIII to defend the Solent. It became the chief operation centre for the Second World War D Day Landings.

The famous Round the Island Race attracts hundreds of entries. I would like to enter next year, hopefully on my even older Laser, when the combined age of Boat and Helmsman will be 87.

I noticed a couple of 35 - 40 footers tacking back and forth against the tide, but not making any headway, so I decided to keep in tight to the IOW coast, not more than 200 yards before tacking back. At least I was making some progress. Within an hour the tide turned so I was able to sail quite quickly to Lymington.

There were big seas running out of the channel where it narrows past Hurst Castle, which was built by Henry VIII in 1544 as a blockhouse. As I turned north westward, the big waves swamped Oops and capsized her. Fortunately we were drifting into slightly calmer waters, so I was able to right her fairly easily, and now I am not tacking, as I head past Milford on Sea, Barton on

Sea, Highcliffe, Mudeford, and round Hengisbury Head, where a hoard of 3000 second century coins were uncovered, which had been minted by the local Iron Age inhabitants.

Archaeologists have found traces of the earliest communities in Britain, a camp of Reindeer hunters, about 11,000 years old. The wind died just before Boscombe, so I called it a day.

As I pulled Oops up to the Prom I realised that high tide would come half way up the wall, so I had to attach a long rope and tie it to the railings, and hope it wouldn't bump about too much. I then had to find a reasonable place to camp which I did behind some beach huts, on a rough piece of ground. I don't like to do this - leaving things away from the boat, as I feel it is less likely to be stolen if it's tied roughly inside the well. The boat still leaks, but not as much as yesterday, so I will carry on tomorrow until I can find a yacht chandler. I'm OK for a meal in a pub tonight but unable to get anything for breakfast or lunch tomorrow apart from a Mars bar.

Friday May 7th
Another early start, 7.30, and I shot across the bay to Studland Bay, past Bournemouth, and my favourite Poole Harbour, one of the largest shallow water anchorages in Britain, and like Sydney Harbour has one of the longest natural harbour shorelines in the world at an amazing 100 miles. In the middle is Brownsea Island where Baden Powell held a camp for 20 boys in 1907, out of which grew the worldwide Scout movement.

I then went past Old Harry Rock which is quite impressive when seen from close quarters from below. We have often walked around this part of the coast, and it's great to get a different (but just as spectacular) view. I thought about stopping at Swanage, but as I was going so well decided to carry on round Durlston Head. As I got to the large waves off the headland I realised I wasn't actually making any progress. It's strange as you plough through the waves, you think you're going great guns, until you look at the land, and see you are going nowhere.

I looked back to see a couple of boats leaving the Swanage sailing club, so I turned back to ask their advice about tides around here. There were a few people at the clubhouse, and they wanted me to sign their visitor's book, after I told them why I was there. What a great club.

1) The sailors advised me that the tide would turn about 1.30,
2) Bill had some resin and fibre glass matting which he helped me fix the leak with,
3) I had a brill all day breakfast in the local café, and
4) I got some food for the next couple of days.

So that's four birds with one stone.

I waited until 2.00 for the resin to set really hard.

With good luck wishes from the club members, this time I shot round Durlston Head, where there is the Great Sphere - a 40 ton Portland stone inscribed with a map of the world. Then past the square stone chapel built in 1150, at the tip of St. Albans Head, which is very impressive. On Lulworth (without being shot at by the army), and the arch of white limestone at Durdle Door. I then headed south missing the huge Portland Harbour and Weymouth, to the Bill of Portland.

Portland is a massive Limestone island, and the limestone has been used in St. Paul's, and the Tower of London. It was also used in the United Nations Headquarters in New York. Great tidal races run off the tip of the Bill, with currents of up to seven knots, so I had to be pretty careful not to screw anything up here. Fortunately I still had the tide with me, so once I was round the tip, I came about and got a fantastic reach for three miles, right up the western side of Portland, and came ashore at the beginning of Chesil Beach at Fortuneswell.

I tried to haul Oops up onto the steep shore of huge rounded stones. Tricky this, I can't use the fender, because if I let go, it slides back into the sea. Fortunately a fisherman saw my plight and came to help. What a brilliant day, I made 50miles, cured the leak and had a hot meal – can't be bad. Mind you it was getting late and once I had phoned Hilary, and got to a pub it was too late to order a meal, so I went back to put the tent up in the dark (I must eat more carrots), then I had another all-day breakfast, but this time out of a tin.

So that's the end of my first week, and I am just over two days behind my original schedule.

CHAPTER 3

FORTUNESWELL TO GORAN HAVEN

<u>Saturday May 8th</u>
I slept through the shipping forecast at 5.45 so I had to guess, and my guess was that the wind was stronger than I would have liked, but if I could get at least eight miles to the other end of Chesil Beach, the beaches are more user friendly for landing and launching. (Chesil is very steep at both high and low tides). I launched OK at 8.30 and found it hard going against the wind and the tide. I capsized within the first half hour, but soon righted her and carried on.
About an hour and one and a half miles further on, an RNLI lifeboat approached and a crew member asked if I was OK, and had I capsized earlier. I said yes to both, but they wanted to know my intentions for the day, who my land based contact is, and would I ring the Coastguard when I land. Apparently a few people had seen me capsize and phoned 999 to tell the Coastguard.
The RNLI were called out but couldn't find me at first, as I was further along the coast from the capsize siting. They weren't happy but waved goodbye and I continued along the coast for another mile or so, only to be confronted by a red flag and an Army chap waving frantically for me to land. I didn't really want to do this as the breaking waves were getting bigger as the wind was increasing. I came close a couple of times and he shouted to me saying I wasn't allowed to pass, so I reluctantly landed heavily, fortunately with no damage done. He told me that the Army was firing here across the Fleet river and there is a one and a half kilometre exclusion zone off the beach, and a kilometre along the beach. "I can't hear any firing" I said. "Oh, no when we saw you nearing the flag we stopped firing" he said. "So if I had continued, you wouldn't have started firing till I was past the next flag in about fifteen minutes time" I replied "That's right" he said. There was still no firing - now 20 minutes after I had landed. Don't lose your temper Ron. "OK so I'll sail one and a half kilometres offshore, then along one kilometre, and then back in. Is that OK?" I asked "Yes" he replied. "What if I misjudge, and only get say one and a quarter kilometres offshore before changing direction and go back into your patch?" I asked "Oh that's OK we will track you on the Radar, and stop firing if you get anywhere near the imaginary line" he replied. Sounds fine to me, I'll have a go - what a great system!
I quickly turned Oops round and tried to launch, but the large breaking

waves nearly capsized her, and the boom dug into the stones, spun her round, and ripped the sail from batten pocket to mast. At the same time I must have head-butted something, because my glasses are smashed to bits. The Army chap was obviously bored by now and he went back to his war games while I spent the next half an hour dragging Oops above the high tide line.

What to do now? One side is the sea, the other side a drop to the river Fleet, with no shelter. I can't go northwards as that is where the army are playing, so I guess I'll go south. First though I packed the ripped sail and made sure the first spare is OK.

So, now I had to walk back towards Portland. It was hard going on these stones carrying three bags, but after half a mile I spotted an old fishing hut near the river. Perhaps I could pitch the tent on the lee side. Success, the stones are slightly smaller here, and it's now only a three mile walk back to civilisation, in guess what - you've got it - the pouring rain.

A couple of beers to calm down, then on the blower to Hilary, who has already had a call from the Coastguards, who think I'm mad, but said that if I have to do it at least phone them every morning and evening, so that they know where I am, and where I'm headed. They sent Hilary, by Email, a list of all the telephone numbers of the Coastguard stations around Britain. I would then be able to pick up the numbers when I found an internet café. They also said that if they get any 999 calls, they can ask if the culprit is me, and if so, have I righted the boat, and am I merrily sailing on my way. I accept that this is a good idea, as I don't want to get the RNLI out on a wild goose chase, and my VHF radio is really only to be used by me to make a "Mayday" call, which I hope I never have to make.

I can also understand that any "non boating types" who see my capsized dinghy may automatically assume that I need rescuing. However, a capsized Laser is not a rare occurrence and I'd like a fiver for every time I was to capsize in the next five months.

I phoned the Coastguards to confirm my understanding of what they want me to do, I was given a bit of a lecture about how dangerous it was, that I should be wearing a lifejacket, instead of a buoyancy aid, and that I should be carrying flares. I accepted that maybe I should buy some mini flares, but explained that I wear a wet suit as well as a buoyancy aid, and that to wear a lifejacket would mean that every time I capsized, they would have to rescue me as I couldn't right the boat looking like a Michelin Man. I should have asked why, neither they, nor the RNLI didn't mention the fact that I was just about to go through the Army exclusion zone earlier today, but thought I would let that one slide.

I managed to buy some Cordon Bleu food (in tins) and a couple of beers (in tins), and trudged back to my five star camp site in the pouring rain. What joy! For a while today I thought about giving up this silly project, but as Henry Ford once said "whether you think you can, or think you can't - you are right". I must keep thinking "I can." An agnostic can do anything if he doesn't know whether to believe in anything or not.

Sunday May 9th
The rain eased and the wind died, and I had a fairly comfortable night, so up at 8.00 and raring to go, but what's this - can I see a red flag - yes - so I trudged up the beach and spoke to a different Army lookout. "I heard about you, but we will be finished about 1400 hours" he said, just as it started to rain. As there was very little wind, I could see no point in beating out past their imaginary line so I went back to the tent, and had another few hours' kip.
Chesil Beach is a weird place, for a million years pebbles have been thrown onto this 18 mile natural breakwater, sorted by size. They start off three and a half inches at Portland and just less that one inch at Abbotsbury. Smugglers and fishermen landing here could estimate their position to within 250 yards, by the size of the stones. It seems incredible that in 1824, a gale carried a ninety five ton sloop right over the beach and plonked it into the Fleet.
I left at 2.00, after phoning the Coastguard, sailed past Abbotsbury where the Benedictine monks kept what still is the largest Swannery in England to provide them with food. I only managed to get to Swyre, when the wind died completely at about 6.00, so I paddled ashore. I had only managed ten miles in the last two days, and am now nearly four days behind schedule, after only nine days.
I estimate I have done 160 miles, although my GPS says I am 122 miles from home as the crow flies. I pulled Oops up above high tide mark and found a nice sheltered spot to camp in a springy, grassy field, after the obligatory 2 phone calls - one to Hilary, and one to the Coastguards.
Then it was off to the Black Bull for turkey and all the trimmings. (I was hoping for roast Swan, but I don't think the Queen is keen on letting us plebs have any). Walking back in the dark, I slipped and managed to land in an ankle deep muddy puddle, so now my "land" shoes are as wet and smelly as my "sea" shoes.

Monday May 10th
The forecast is a northerly force 2 to 3. I started off well, past Charmouth, where Danish pirates landed and slaughtered many people in AD831. The cliffs here are famous for their fossils, and in 1811, a twenty one foot ichthyosaurus was found here. On past Lyme Regis, with its massive stone

Cobb - the thousand year old harbour. The wind died and I struggled to get past Axmouth, which is the sea terminus of the Roman Fosse Way,
I paddled for a while hoping the wind would pick up, but decided it wasn't going to, and that with a name like Beer, this town just had to be visited. I spotted some dinghies on the beach and hoped there would be a sailing club, where I could get a shower at last. Success - they were racing that evening and a couple of people were working on their boats. I asked if there was a yacht chandler anywhere, and one of the guys said there was one about two miles away, and insisted on taking me in his car.
I managed to get some flares that can be seen up to ten miles away at night, and five miles during the day. I also tried on a couple of lifejackets, but as I suspected, it would be impossible to right the laser when it was fully inflated. The driver was interested in my story and when we got back to the club, introduced me to other club members, and we had a few beers. He even offered me a bed for the night, but I declined the offer as I wanted to leave early and, also, I don't like to leave the laser unattended all night. I was to get a few kind offers like this, but only spent two nights in proper beds, the whole adventure.

Tuesday May 11th
Still light winds but I left at 8.00 and made good progress until I got to Budleigh Salterton, where I hung around for an hour and a half going nowhere. I limped along to Exmouth and then to Dawlish as the fogbanks were rolling in. This was getting scary as I could hear the occasional train, and the waves breaking on the shore, but I couldn't see anything. I nearly bumped into a couple of extraordinary stacks off Holcombe called The Parson and Clerk.
I decided to land at Teignmouth with the compass as my only friend - quite frightening. If you can remain calm while all around you is chaos - then you probably haven't completely understood the seriousness of the situation. As I hauled up on the beach, out of the gloom a man walked with his dog. I asked him to confirm that I was in fact in Teignmouth. My map shows the railway turning inland here and as I hadn't heard a train for some time, it was possible that I had got further south-west than I thought. The guy confirmed this but was surprised that I wasn't sure. This was to happen a few times in the future - quite embarrassing really.
My GPS is now out of action - it got waterlogged yesterday, and although I have dried it and tried new batteries it still won't work. Oh well, it's cheaper to ask someone where the hell I am rather than buy a new one. I don't use it whilst sailing anyway - I don't have enough hands.

Wednesday May 12th

It looks like another slow day with a south westerly force 3 to 4, but it seemed much less. I ghosted to the end of Babbacombe Bay, round Hope's Nose, and past Thatcher Rock into Tor Bay. I decided to stay well out in the bay and head straight for Berry Head at the eastern side of Brixham.

This was England's premier fishing port for 300 years, until about a hundred years ago with the famous Brixham Trawlers - powerful fishing smacks that could sail far afield in search of fish for the tables of London. Those days are over and now there are only a few motor trawlers left. They do however commemorate the great days of sail with a race round the bay in June annually.

The lighthouse at Berry Head is the shortest, the highest, and the deepest in England. The shortest because it's lens is only six feet above ground level. The highest because it stands on a headland higher than any other above sea level and deepest because it has a thirty foot pit which houses the clockwork weights by which it is driven.

I continued slowly past Cod Rock (I wonder how it got that name), towards Scabbacombe Head, where a seal popped up about two feet behind me and breathed - it frightened the life out of me. This was the first real encounter with wildlife, but certainly won't be the last. The wind was dying as I went past Mew Stone, and I had to paddle into Dartmouth, past the Castle to the first pink house on the left, where John Polley was to put me up for the night. He was one of the few to respond to my letter in Yachts and Yachting, and is keen to do a similar adventure on his catamaran. He had a few ideas that we discussed. He is a leading light at the local Sailing Club, where we went, and I signed their visitors' book, and bent the old elbow a few times. Now John's a great bloke but he would keep trying to sit on my shoulder, and talk about pieces of eight. I seem to remember having a Pizza (I managed to avoid having a pavement pizza) then we got stuck into the brandy back at his place, which I was to regret the next day.

Thursday May 13th

I was up later than usual (taking advantage of a proper bed). The old head was pounding a bit, but after a leisurely breakfast on a real chair, at a real table, I set off. John escorted me out of the harbour in his canoe. With all these light winds he is faster than me - perhaps that's the answer to my next challenge????

I slowly sailed through Start Bay, round the lighthouse at Start Point, and on to Salcombe, where Tennyson anchored off the Bar in his yacht *Sunbeam* in 1889, and was inspired to write his famous poem "Crossing the Bar".

I had just decided to give up for the day when the wind picked up, so I carried on past Bolt Head, then on to Hope Cove, where in 1760, the 90-gun warship HMS Ramillies foundered on the rocks, losing 800 lives (so not much hope there then). Then it was on past Bigbury Bay, and on to Wembury Bay, where I hauled up onto a beach just as it was getting dark, near some caravans. I thought it was a camp site, but it was just a static caravan site with no facilities.

I walked about a mile but couldn't find a pub, so I asked at a house, and was told that the nearest pub was three miles away. I asked if I could buy half a loaf of bread, but the chap wouldn't let me pay and also donated £5 for the charity. Then I trudged back to the beach, put the tent up in the dark, and cooked macaroni cheese, out of a tin, by torch-light - luxury.

Friday May 14th

Today's forecast is south westerly force 2 to 3, which seems a bit optimistic to me as I float about going virtually nowhere, until lunch time. It started off alright past Plymouth, where Drake played his legendary game of bowls, round Rame Head, along Whitsand Bay.

I had to go to the loo, so I pulled up onto the beach at Looe, rushed into the public loos only to find that all the loo seats had been stolen. The police had been informed, but they had to drop the case, as they had nothing to go on! Much relieved I carried on past Polperro, Fowey, and now in a freshening wind, across St Austell Bay, where you can see the big square riggers at Charlestown, on past Mevagissey and into Goran Haven where I landed on a lovely sandy beach, which I had all to myself. I walked into the village and had a proper meal in the local, back to the beach, up with the tent and I was asleep by 9.30 - bliss.

CHAPTER 4

GORAN HAVEN TO PORT ISAAC

Saturday May 15th
I awoke to what looked like being a really hot and still day, I launched and drifted past Dodman Point, where in 1588 the Spanish Armada were formed into battle lines before sailing to meet Drake's fleet. I then went past Porthluney Cove, and an interesting Castle called Caerhays, built in 1808, designed by John Nash, who later designed Marble Arch, and Brighton Pavilion. The cost was so great that the owner ended up really hard up, and the last member of his family was said to have spent his evenings shooting out the eyes of ancestral portraits.

Then it was slowly round Nare Head, the site of Carne Beacon, 370 feet in circumference, one of the largest burial mounds in Britain. Gereint, King of Cornwall is said to be buried here alongside his golden ship. I paddled in to Porth Beach, hoping the wind would pick up, but in the end I walked to the village, stocked up on beer and grub, and sunbathed all afternoon - what's the point of trying to be a hero. I could spend all day on the sea paddling and only make one mile headway. Eagles may soar, but weasels don't get sucked into jet engines.

Sunday May 16th
Another hot and calm day, just right for a wet suit. Still I don't mind it being gentle, if I am to go round the Lizard, which is a notorious headland, the furthest south point on the British mainland. I launched about 8.00 and drifted round Zone point, to the spectacular view of Falmouth, which saw more shipping than any other port except London from Tudor times to the end of the 19th century. In 1815 three hundred and fifty ships were counted in Garrick Roads on one day. I saw only five or six large vessels, which were impressive, but just imagine 350 large sailing merchant ships. Then on past Helford and Frenchman's Creek, made famous by Daphne du Maurier, in the novel about a dashing and daring pirate.

At Gillan harbour, the 15th century Church of St. Anthony had a tower built in thanksgiving of shipwrecked Normans, who returned with the fine grained granite only found in Normandy. The emblem of the church is a pig, and people of the parish are called St. Anthony pigs. A celebration is held in December called the Piggy Feast.

I started to make good progress as the gentle breeze is now behind me. As it is so calm, the water is like a millpond but suddenly it seemed to boil as a large shoal of fish started moving about, chased by a couple of dolphins, and then lots of sea birds arrived for breakfast. Everything happens at once, then I drift away and all is calm again.

I was getting uncomfortably hot for the first time whilst afloat in my wet suit, so I managed to struggle out of the bolero top and carried on with just a tee shirt on top. I went in between Godrevy Cove, and The Manacles, which is a cluster of forbidding rocks, which have wrecked hundreds of ships. Their name derives from "Maen Eglos", Cornish for stone church. St, Keverne's graveyard, close by has more than 400 shipwrecked victims buried there.

Then it was on past Black Head (that reminds me I must pick one later), and so to the Lions Den, an enormous cave whose roof collapsed in 1847. The swell is really getting big here, and as I drifted towards The Lizard, a sudden gybe nearly caught me out, as the boom just missed my head. I headed further south, so that I was reaching more, and less likely to gybe again. Once I was past the Lizard, I came about and headed north, again on more of a reach, so I still wasn't in danger of gybing. I wish now I had my full wet suit on - I don't fancy capsizing in this, and although I'm not cold, I can feel the sun burning my arms which have no sun-cream on. As I look up at the lighthouse on top of the 180 feet cliffs, the swell is so great that I can only see it for a few seconds at a time. It's like a white man on a zebra crossing - now you see me, now you don't.

It's the first time I have been in really huge seas on a laser, and I am amazed they can be so big in such calm conditions. You only associate big seas with big winds, but as I am now exposed to the 3000 miles of the Atlantic rushing straight to these shores I suppose I will have to get used to it, as I head towards Lands End and start my northern passage. The lighthouse, here, built in 1752, is one of Britain's brightest, seen up to 21 miles away. The first lighthouse here was built by a pirate landowner, who hoped that ships would see the light, but founder on his land, where he would have rights to any wreckage.

As I get into the relative calm of Kynance Cove, I have time to put my wet suit top back on. You suddenly get a warm feeling of safety, totally illogical, but I always think it's like putting a crash helmet on. The cove has strange sounding outcrops - Asparagus Island, Devil's Postbox, The Devil's Bellows, Steeple Rock and Man-o-War Rock, and two fascinating caves - The Parlour and The Drawing Room. The surf boils between the rocks and crashes into the caves - quite spectacular.

I carry on round Mount's Bay, past The Loe, a lake where King Arthur is said to have flung his sword, past Porthleven, but the wind is again dying, so out with the trusty paddle, and I managed to reach Praa Sands just as it's getting dark. A good day followed by an enormous fish pie in the pub right on the beach, and an early night - shattered.

Monday May 17th
I am a bit apprehensive, as today I should be going round Land's End, one of the worst headlands in Britain, still the forecast is for very light winds, so I should be ok. A slow start, past Cudden Point, then St Michael's Mount came into view - spectacular - a 363 ft granite island topped by a castellated tower, a quarter of a mile offshore - one of Cornwall's principal attractions. Past Penzance, which was sacked by the Spanish in 1595, and most of the buildings destroyed. Then across to Mousehole, pronounced *mowsle,* derived from the Cornish word *maew* (gull) and *holh* (basin). A good reach past Porthcurno, where there is the terminus of eleven ocean cables that once connected Britain to international telephone networks, the first to Bombay was completed in 1870. On the cliffs is a Greek style amphitheatre, with the sea as a backdrop.
I knew that just past here I had to start bearing north westwards towards Land's End, so here goes!!! In the event, a bit of a pussy cat, with little wind, but still with huge seas. So once round Land's End I decided that Sennen Cove would be my best bet to stop for the day, as it's a long way to the next "sensible" beach.
I went round the rocks to the south of the bay, and tried to land in the middle of the bay which was a big mistake. It was fine until 50 feet from land, and then all hell broke loose, as big surfing waves started to break. With no wind, I had no control of the boat, and over she went. The top of the mast dug in the sand, and snap!
A couple of guys saw me struggle and helped drag Oops and what was left of the sail and mast up on the beach. It was so stupid, because I saw the small harbour just past the rocks as I came into the cove, where I could easily land, but thought the sandy beach would be a doddle.
Once I had calmed down I walked to the RNLI station, but the mechanic had gone home for the day, and the chaps assured me that he had a pop rivet gun, and would be able to help in the morning. I went back to the boat and set about repairing the sail, but broke my last needle. So back into the village, where I asked a lady if there was a shop around that could sell me some needles. She said that she works voluntarily for the RNLI, and had heard about my adventure. She had some needles and kindly let me have a whole packet. They were nice big strong needles that she said she would never use anyway, and was pleased to help out. I managed to mend half of the sail before dark, and then I walked a couple of miles to a camp site where they let me use their shower. What a day!

Tuesday May 18th

At 9.00ish I was waiting for Richard (the RNLI mechanic) along with my broken mast and repair kit. When he arrived, he said he had a rivet gun but no rivets, but popped to the shops on his motor bike for some. He had a drill, so we set about doing the repairs, and about half an hour later all was fixed. Thanks Richard, what a diamond geyser. But I now know that it's important I carry my pop rivet gun and rivets, so I made a note to ask Hilary to bring them when she comes to see me at the weekend.

It's not practical for me to carry a drill, but I figure that most houses in Britain will have a drill I can borrow, but a rivet gun is not so common.

Hilary has managed to locate a new sail - a race training sail that is virtually the same as a proper one, but as it is not made by Lasers, is out of class, and therefore you can't race with it. It is also about half the price, so guess which one I will buy.

So job done, and with a cheery wave to the RNLI guys I trundle back to Oops, where I finished sewing the sail, then for the launch - not so easy as the big surfing waves were still rolling in. By 1.00 I'm ready to go, and I managed to press-gang 4 lads, sunbathing, into carrying Oops along the beach nearer to the small harbour, where the breaking waves were smaller.

I launched and sailed into the harbour, so I could sort everything out, and get lined up to sail across the bay in the large swell. Slowly past Aire Point, over the huge waves (up and down, like a whore's drawers), past a small island called the Brinsons, and Cape Cornwall - the only Cape in England. I doubt if it's as big or frightening as Scotland's Cape Wrath. Once I rounded Pendeen Watch, I again ran out of wind, and realised that Portheras Cove was the only place to land for the next ten miles, so there was no point in trying to get to St. Ives with no wind. The only trouble was that there were lots of big rocks, and as it was high tide, with quite a steep shoreline, I decided to stand off for a while and hope the breaking waves would quieten down.

I waited a couple of hundred yards off, and now and then paddled to get closer to the shore, but it was three hours before I thought it would be OK to get through the breaking waves. Here goes – fortunately, I got it right this time and flew up the beach on a fairly small breaking wave. I was greeted by four people who had been watching me, and couldn't understand what I was doing. They speculated as to whether I had died, and was just drifting about! They were at the point of going to use the emergency phone to speak to the Coastguard, when I finally decided to try for a landing. They were camping rough on the top of the cliffs and I joined them with their catch of fish, and some bread. If they thought I was going to turn their water into wine, they were going to be disappointed. I was a bit worried about how I was going to get off the next day, as I can't seem to do much with so little wind, and if the wind does pick up, normally the sea gets even bigger. Oh well, lets not worry about that until tomorrow.

Wednesday May 19th
Oh dear, still no wind, but let's attempt to launch. I failed to get through the breaking surf on the first four attempts, so decided to wait for low tide. I chatted to my new friends - me in full wet suit, and them in just shorts. At low tide I made another attempt, and made it this time, but with furious paddling, it still took an hour to get out of sight of the bay.
I paddled and drifted, drifted and paddled, and after what seemed like a lifetime, and four miles later I managed to creep into St. Ives just as a sea breeze sprang up. Bugger me!!!! Still at least I can land on a lee shore with no big breakers. There is a granite quay here, built in 1767 by John Smeaton, who also built the first successful Eddystone Lighthouse.
I must try and pick my bays, or better still harbours, more carefully along this coast. I didn't realise just how big the seas get coming straight off 3,000 miles of the Atlantic. We don't see anything like it at Eastbourne, and I suppose I am a bit naïve to expect the same as at home.
Still I had made it to a town, so Cornish Pasties and a few beers are the order of the day. I phoned Hilary, and finalised my list of items for Oops that she and my son Ian are bringing for me at the weekend. I was hoping to get further up the Bristol Channel, so it was not as far for them to come, but such is life.
When I got back to the beach, I joined in with an impromptu Barbie (that's a BBQ - not Ken's friend). Half a dozen people had lit a fire on the beach near to Oops. I couldn't just put up the tent and go to bed, so I joined them as they had some beers and sausages that they insisted on sharing. What a great night.

Thursday May 20th
I started at 7.00 in light winds, and sailed straight across St. Ives Bay, then got stuck tacking back and forth trying to get past the Godrevy Lighthouse. After about two hours, I started making headway, and picked up a message on my mobile from the Coastguard who had a call from someone thinking I was in trouble, as I wasn't going anywhere. I told them I was OK, just stuck in light airs.
The wind was at last picking up, but from the North East, so I am now beating into it, just like I was all the way along the south coast. I am now making good progress though, past all the abandoned tin mining enginehouses, past St.Agnes, where John Opie the painter was born in 1761, and where the miners cottages are called the "stippy-stappy". Then it was on past

Perranporth, and the big surfing beach, past Holywell Bay, Porth Joke (known locally as Polly Joke), Fistral Bay, and finally round Towan Head, and into Newquay Bay, where I had difficulty getting into the harbour, as it is exposed to these north easterly winds. I had to keep reaching back and forth against the waves until I could just pop into the entrance, and immediately gybe in the now relative calm of the harbour.

I went into the sailing club, but they didn't even have a shower, so I settled for a beer and then found the local public loos where I had my usual strip wash in cold water again. At least I can warm up afterwards in one of the many pubs serving excellent beer and pasties.

In the pub I overheard a guy saying to his wife "Shall we change positions tonight". She replied "OK, you stand next to the iron all night and I'll sit on the sofa, watching the TV and farting".

Friday May 21st
I decided to have a lie in as I wanted to go at low tide, so that the flooding current would push me northward. I am already in the strong pull of the Bristol Channel, where there is no mucking about with strange currents; it's either strong north-east (flood) or strong south-west (ebb). I spoke to the local fishermen, who told me that if I didn't get out of the harbour two hours before low tide, I would have to drag the boat out into the bay, and launch from the beach in (guess what?) huge waves.

I looked over the harbour wall, and knew that I wouldn't be able to launch in that lot, so quickly got ready, and launched in the harbour, before the sea receded too far. This meant that for the next two hours I only managed about half a mile.

However once the tide turned, I got moving, even though there was little wind, and big lumpy seas. Then I went past Watergate Bay (Nixon's favourite bay) where in 1869 the ship Suez was driven ashore. It is said that some of the rescuers insisted on only using the Newquay rowing boat to rescue the seamen, instead of the steam tug, so they could plunder the Suez when it became wrecked. Unfortunately for them the steam tug came out anyway and towed the ship to safety, causing a fight.

I carried on past Redruthan Steps where a rocky pinnacle known as Queen Bess stands. It is said to present a profile of Queen Elizabeth I, complete with ruff and farthingale. I couldn't see it myself. What vivid imagination the Cornish have. (Either that or someone's been at the rum again). I carried on around Trevose Head, through even bigger seas, and towards Padstow Bay, where I originally intended to stop for the night. As the sea still had such a big swell, I didn't fancy going past the Doom Bar, across the harbour entrance, where the lifeboats have saved 500 lives since 1825, because of the fierce currents, and unpredictable local winds. I decided to go round Pentire Point, Rumps Point, on past Kellan Head, and made for Port Isaac. I had the same problem as yesterday, getting into the harbour, reaching back and forth, until a lull in the big waves, allowed me to dive in, and quickly gybe, then gently up the beach in the relative calm, behind the harbour wall.

As I went to get some food, I saw a man carrying a scaffold pole. I said "are you a pole vaulter." He said "No, I am German, but how did you know my name is Volter."

CHAPTER 5

PORT ISAAC TO LITTLE HAVEN

Saturday May 22nd
I will be meeting Ian and Hilary today, who are driving down with my new sail, new self bailer, and various extras that I need especially my rivet gun.
So up early and see if I can make it to Bude. Once round Land's End, the south westerly winds should be pushing me along nicely, but guess what, it's a north easterly. So off I go again tacking all the way. I can see the spectacular Tintagel Castle from just outside Port Isaac harbour, about five miles away.
All the hype about this Castle being King Arthur's pad is amazing, when you consider that it was built in 1145, some 600 years after King Arthur led the Celts against the invading Saxons. It was Tennyson's poems that popularised the idea that Arthur was ever here. Still, it is a lovely romantic spot, and a prosperous King Arthur "industry" was established years ago, and plenty of people are still reaping the benefit.
I carried on beating past Tintagel Head, and Bossiney Haven, where for centuries it had its' own Mayor, and Sir Francis Drake was an MP here in the 16th Century. Then I went past The Meachard, protecting Boscastle, which has since had a horrendous flash flood. Then past The Strangles, which are jagged rocks, just off the coast, where in the 1820's 23 vessels were wrecked.
I made it past Widemouth Sands and on to Bude at just about low tide. Not a good time to arrive, as it took ages dragging Oops up to the high tide line, past the Lifeguards, who looked but didn't volunteer any help. I phoned Hilary first in the hope that they may be in the vicinity and would be able to help. I think they were at the top of the beach all the time, hiding until I made it all the way up. Apparently Ian and Hilary had gone to Tintagel to see if they could see me en route, which they didn't. It was great to see them again, but I was surprised that Tina hadn't come. Hilary had left her with Lisa, Hilary's neice. I was then whisked off to the lap of luxury - a camp site at last. After a shower, a couple of beers, and a decent meal I felt like a new man. But where could I find one at this time of night?

Sunday May 23rd
We spent a nice lazy morning, but as Hilary and Ian had to get back home, I decided at lunch time to do a few jobs on Oops as I had some help. As it was low tide (again), it was nice to have some help as all three of us lugged Oops down to the water's edge, still with the Lifeguards looking on.

I left with an emotional farewell at 3.00. It could be ages before I will see them again, and I have some pretty inhospitable coastlines to negotiate before I do. Looking at the map I can see that there are few options for a landing later on. But I am making steady progress against the wind, past Higher Sharpnose Point. The cliff tops here are about 500-600 feet, with very few landing places. As I get near to Hartland Point I can see why it is has a reputation as one of the most frightening headlands in the West Country. It is estimated that the force of a wave crashing against the rocks averages 2000lb. per square foot in winter. Ptolemy described it as "The Promontory of Hercules". I'm just glad the weather is relatively calm today. Ian and Hilary were at Hartland Quay waiting three hoursto see me sail by. Apparently they were shouting and waving furiously in the hope I would see them, but I was oblivious to it all, as I thought they were already driving home. At least the people at Hartland Quay had some entertainment for the day!!

As I round the point, I realise that I am making no headway against the ebb. As it is getting late, I crept in close to shore, hopefully out of the main current. I can see a small bay, called Shipload Bay, which doesn't look very inviting, but will have to do. There is nowhere else until Clovelly, in five miles, and even then I don't know what the landing will be like, although I know there is a small jetty there.

I landed OK, but had to haul Oops up over huge rocks until I got to the high tide mark, adding dozens more scratches to her bottom. The next job was to climb up the cliff, to get a signal on the phone. The area around here is owned by the National Trust, but the wooden steps down to the shore have been washed away, so a bit of mountain climbing is required. Up on the cliff there are "Danger - keep out" signs which I will have to ignore on my way back, once I have made my obligatory phone calls. Success, only a one mile hike until I got a signal, then it is back to the rocky beach to figure out where to sleep for the night. I toyed with the idea of propping the boat into a reasonable position, to lay on it, but couldn't get a six foot length that would do, without a fitting or shackle digging in. I scoured the beach, and found a flattish rock with a 20 degree slope. I laid down on it and found it OK, but my feet and legs overhung the end. So up with the tent, that overhung all four corners, a quick all day breakfast out of a tin, and hoped to god I didn't roll off onto the rocks below overnight.

Monday May 24th
I had a fairly disturbed night, subconsciously not trying to move too much. How mountaineers kip in tents like this clinging to rock faces, I don't know. And they sometimes have to stay in them for days on end when the weather

claggs in.

The weather here though was fairly calm, but I could see the tide going out, and thought it best to leave quickly, with as little damage as possible to Oops over the rocks. I will come back here one day and put up the tent again to take a photo - it is the worse place for a camp site on the whole trip, and such an apt name - Shipload Bay.

I fought the ebbing tide for about two hours, with virtually no wind, so I decided to land about 200 yards from where I started, and kept pulling the boat back to the deep water over the rocks every 10 minutes as the tide receded. What I really needed was a reverse King Canute, to stop the tide going out. I managed to do one or two jobs on Oops, had some tea and sandwiches, then it was off as the tide turned and the flood should whisk me up the Bristol Channel. Whisk isn't quite the right word, but at least I was making progress, past Clovelly, with its quaint cottages painted in bright colours.

Then past Westward Ho, named after Charles Kingsley's novel about Elizabethan sailors. Rudyard Kipling went to the United Services College here between 1878 and 1882, and based his book *Stalky and Co.* on his experiences here. Past Saunton Sands, Croyde Bay, and Baggy Point, where I have been rock climbing in the past. It was here in 1799 that HMS Weasle was wrecked with the loss of 105 lives. On past Morte Bay and Woolacombe where the sea was getting bigger and out to Morte Point, where the sea was getting frighteningly bigger. What an apt name Morte Point - where 18th century wreckers tied lanterns to the horns of cows on the hillside, so that sailors would mistake the lights for Ilfracombe, and be lured onto the rocks. I decided to land as it was getting dark, and the wind had died again, so just past Bull Point, I spotted a small cove called Lee Bay. That would do nicely - no big rocks here! I pulled Oops right up near to the road, changed and went in search of refreshments. In the local hotel they had beer, but it was too late to order food, so armed with a full pint glass, it was back to the beach, where I cooked yet another All Day Breakfast (tinned).

It was still early so I took my glass back to the hotel, had another pint and played crib with a local, who told me that his son had came home early from school one day, and caught him in bed with his wife. - "Wot yer doin Dad" - "Playing crib and your mum is my partner". So the boy went into the shed, where his Grandad usually hides, and asked "Wot yer doin Grandad", who replied "Playing crib". "Where's yer partner?" the boy asked. Grandad replied "With a hand like this you don't need a partner."

Tuesday May 25th

Whilst listening to the shipping forecast at 5.45, I started doing some sums and decided that today was the day to bite the bullet and go straight across the Bristol Channel to Wales. The wind had turned to a south westerly at last, and although not very strong, was still a good force three, but easing later. The only problem was that I couldn't actually see Wales as it is about 25 miles away.

I spoke to the Swansea coastguard, who said he could clearly see Ilfracombe, (about two miles from where I am) through his binoculars, as the cliffs are much higher here than Swansea. The tide would flood up into the Bristol Channel, until about 11.00, and then should help me as it ebbed south westwards for another six hours. If I leave early, I will have all day to make it across, and may get even further westward than Swansea. As I was about to leave, some Hotel guests came down with some donations for my charity - they had heard about my challenge last night, and couldn't believe I was actually camping on the beach, let alone trying for Wales today.

By the time I was ready to go at about 7.30, there were about twenty people on the beach cheering me off. What a great send off for what was to be a very scary day. The sun was shining, the seas were fairly benign, and for the first two hours I kept looking back to see the cliff tops, which was a comfort. The rest of the time my eyes were glued to the compass (my only friend) to make sure I was heading due north. Gradually I started to think that I could see a mark on the horizon - could I really see anything or was it an optical illusion? Eventually I was sure that there was something there. If I looked behind, then scanned my eyes westward, northward, eastward, then back northward, I could definitely make out something. If only I had some binoculars I would be sure.

After another two hours Wales looked about as clear as England, and I felt confident enough to head North West, and further along the coast from Swansea. I had no idea how far eastward the flooding tide had taken me - all I knew was that the ebb was now taking me westwards. As I got nearer the coast, I tried to figure out landmarks from my map. Was that Mumbles Head? Or was it Oxwich Point? Could it be Porteynon Point?

As the wind was dying, I thought, I don't care - just let's land and work it out later. Still a mile or so off, and out with the paddle. I'm aiming for a headland with what looks like a lot of sea behind it. Can it be Carmarthen Bay, and could the headland I'm looking at be Worm's Head. As I get closer I'm convinced that it is, but as it's now five o'clock, the tide is turning, and I can feel that I am being pulled eastwards again. Frantic paddling, and much blowing on the sail followed - (I must eat more beans). At last I'm round the headland, but what's this - of course, low tide in Rhossili Bay means - sand, sand, and more sand. Still, what the hell, I'm alive and well. What's a few thousand feet dragging Oops up the beach, when you have just made up seven days on the schedule? I am now back to my original estimate, so perhaps I won't be spending Christmas at sea after all.

It took about an hour and a half to get to the high tide line. I haven't worked out the best way of doing it. I tend to carry two bags up, then the sail still attached to the mast. Then it's back to the wheelbarrow technique on the hull, this is fine for the first ten or so times, then I get a bit knackered, and need a rest. This is about the time that someone walks by but doesn't offer a helping hand, so it's back for another ten etc. etc. Once I got everything sorted above high tide line, it was off to the pub, but today I'm in time to order food, so it's a big gammon steak, and a few pints - bliss.

I was definitely on a high when I spoke to Hilary and the Coastguard that night on the blower.

Wednesday May 26th

I had a lie in as high tide will not be until 12.00 and there is very little wind. I don't fancy dragging Oops all the way to the water's edge, and there is no point in trying to sail against the flood. So I walked to the campsite at the other end of the beach, but couldn't find any officials, and decided that they wouldn't mind me having a shower.

Then it was back to the village to get some food, and launched just about high tide. Although there is little wind, I know that the tide will be with me for the next six hours.

I started off on a north westerly course, Heading for Pendine Sands, where the World Land Speed Record was broken five times in the 1920's, the last one being by Sir Malcolm Campbell in Bluebird at 174.88mph, in 1927. As I came close, I could see Caldy Island to my left, and decided to head slightly to the right of it, to try and reach Tenby, before the tide turned. Caldy Island is a fascinating place where Trappist Cistercian Monks sell perfume made from flowers and herbs. A bit cockeyed really, as only men are allowed to visit the monastery, dating back to the 12th Century. Perhaps that's why all the Taff's I have known smell like they do.

I got to Tenby at about 5.30, with the wind dying again, so I knew there was no point in trying to go further with the tide against me as well. The Tenby Sailing Club were having their mid-week race (albeit in dead calm seas) so I went in search of a shower at their club house. It's great, knowing that all these clubs welcome you with open arms, but the only problem is that most are closed five or six days a week. The BBQ was being fired up, so after a shower, I had a great evening, with lots of money being raised by the club members, for which I am very grateful.

Thursday May 27th

Again a lie in as it needs to be high tide before setting sail. I managed a proper breakfast, did some shopping and found the library, where I could send some e-mails. Then it was back to the beach, and the inevitable phone call to the Coastguard.

I left about 11.30, and all was going well, until an Army safety vessel approached from behind, just after I had passed Stackpole Head. He came right up to my transom, and the crew member asked where I was going. I told him I was intending to go as far as Milford Haven or beyond. He told me that I was in a firing range, but I told him that the Coastguard never mentioned it. He then came too close and trapped my back, between his bows and my transom. I said "what are you doing" (or words to that effect), but got no reply. He then backed off and I shouted to him to let me know what he wanted me to do. Again I got no reply so I carried on, on the same course, with this boat about 200 yards behind. I kept waving to them to come close, as my back was now quite painful, but after a while, the boat suddenly turned and disappeared back towards Tenby, without a single word or apology.

I assumed I was now past the firing range, as I came around Linney Head so I carried on. I knew there were no safe landing places until right inside Milford Haven, and when I got around Sheep Island, I could see the place was alive with Tankers and big ferries. I didn't fancy mixing it with these big buggers so I thought it best to go straight across the harbour entrance to St. Ann's Head, and see if I could find a lee shore. I went inside Skokholm Island and Skomer Island, both owned by the Wales Naturalists Trust, where thousands of sea birds, Buzzards and Ravens live. I could see the huge surfing waves crashing on to Marloes Sands, so I knew I had to go much further to have any chance of a safe landing.

Once I got past Martin's Haven, things calmed down a bit, but I didn't like the look of the rocky coastline, until I spotted Little Haven, and a nice sandy beach.

I beached the boat, and was just tentatively pulling the mast out, when my back went click and locked up. I dropped the mast on the sand, and sat against the boat for a while, hoping the pain would ease. As I tried to move I realised that I wasn't going to be able to drag Oops in as the tide was in full flood, so I had no alternative but to ring 999 on my trusty mobile. An ambulance, the Coastguard, along with the Police soon arrived (how embarrassing).

The ambulance whisked me to hospital, and the Coastguards carried Oops up the beach. After a couple of hours of prodding and poking, the doctor decided that it was only pulled tendons or ligaments, and sent me on my way with the inevitable bunch of tablets. I got a taxi back to Little Haven, and set about putting up the tent - no mean feat with a bad back. I found that if I knelt on the beach and did everything from that position it wasn't too bad. It was getting late by this time, but I managed to get a meal in the local, which fortunately was only 100 yards away.

Friday May 28th
I had a terrible night's sleep, but took some more pain killers at about 6.30, and slept right through until 10.30. Obviously there would be no sailing for me today.
I phoned the Coastguards and asked why they did not tell me that I would be passing through the firing range, as I have been told that they get the firing times from the Army. They told me that they don't have a "Duty of Care", and it is up to me to find out. OK so where best to find out - Yep - The Coastguards, I would say. Silly me thinking that they would volunteer it without me asking. I managed to walk to Broad Haven for fish and chips, where I spotted an article in The Mechanics Monthly magazine. It was about a chap in a mental health ward who raped a cleaner and then escaped. The headlines read - "Nut screws washer and bolts".

CHAPTER 6

LITTLE HAVEN TO WALLASEY

<u>Saturday May 29th</u>
I had another painful night. The backache seems to ease if I move about so I may as well be sailing, as long as I keep taking the painkillers. Although the wind wasn't very strong, it was behind me all day, so I managed to knock up quite a few miles. It was easy going across St Brides Bay, and I spotted a couple of dolphins in the distance. By tapping the hull, they suddenly turned towards me to investigate what I am doing. They stayed with me for a few minutes until they decided that I am no fun, and they can't eat me, so they carried on their original direction.
Past Solva, where The Quay was built in 1861, to handle stone for the Smalls Lighthouse, 15 miles offshore. It is one of the most isolated Lighthouses in the world, and in 1800, one of the two keepers died, and his companion was unable to attract attention, so he used the living room panels to make a coffin, which he lashed to the outside of the tower. It was three months until relief came from the mainland. Just thinking about it makes me cringe; the smell of rotting fish is one thing but…...
As I sailed inside Ramsey Island, lots of Puffins were just sitting on the water. As I get to within a few feet they just disappear under the water. They don't dive they just seem to sink. I saw a lot of gannets, and seals basking in the sun on the rocks. What a fantastic day for wildlife. Past St. David's Head, which was named after the Patron Saint of Wales. In AD530 St. David was born in Cardiganshire and after years of travel, spent his later years in this remote corner of Wales. On past Strumble Head, and into Fishguard Bay, where the last invasion of Britain occurred in 1797, when 1200 Napoleonic troops landed here. They were supposed to sack Bristol, but the strong easterly winds forced them here. I'm glad I'm not the only one who isn't quite sure about where I am all the time.
Then it was on to Newport Bay, Ceibwr Bay, round Cardigan Island, and finally I landed at Aberporth. It had a Catamaran Sailing Weekend here, so there was a lot of activity. It was such a busy little bay. There were people with metal detectors, kids throwing rocks at gulls, and fishermen painting boats. So the treasure hunters were leaving no stone unturned, the kids were leaving no tern unstoned, and the fishermen were leaving no stern untoned. There were lots of people camping on the beach, so I didn't feel bad about putting up my tent straight away. Normally I come back to the boat when I'm ready for bed and only put it up then - it feels safer somehow. I managed an

hour's sleep and then went to the pub for a meal, but I still managed to fall asleep at the end of my meal. Someone woke me to see if I was alright, and everyone had a good laugh - how embarrassing.

Sunday May 30th
I left all the cat sailors at about 8.00, they were all asleep, and probably not racing till 11.00, but I have to crack on - none of these wimpy 2 hour races for me.
The light southerly wind was drifting me along the coast past New Quay where Dylan Thomas lived in the 1940's and wrote *Under Milk Wood* here. I saw the play performed in London in the late 1960's by Richard Burton, and Elizabeth Taylor - what a fantastic play, although a little off the wall. This was a really thriving port in the 1860's, and there is a fascinating list on the pier of how much it cost to land artefacts: 5s for a billiard table or barrel organ; 4d for every calf, sheep, pig or fox; 2s for a hundredweight of feathers, and 1s.6d for a marble tombstone.
As I passed the stacks off the coast along here, there was the awful stench of thousands of cormorants, especially as the wind was now nearly non existent, and the smell just lingers on. Most of the cormorants sit with wings laid out drying in the sun, and the rocks are covered in white guano. What would you say to a little shag – "hello little shag".
I resorted to the paddle, and eventually got to Aberystwyth, only to find the sailing club all locked up, so no shower tonight. It really is nice to get a shower, as I have to wear the wet suit all the time I'm sailing, so it's either always full of sea water, or sweat on days like today.

Monday May 31st
The shipping forecast tells me it will be a force 3 to 4, which would be just right as I hope to get across the huge Cardigan Bay to Bardsey Sound today. As I look northwards I can see Bardsey Island towards the north west, so I headed towards it, leaving the land miles behind me. Unfortunately the sky looks threatening and soon it's pouring down, the wind has died and I can't see land anymore, either behind or in front. So much for the shipping forecast.
A bit scary really, but all I can do is watch the compass and hope I'm not drifting too far off course. At times like this I wish I'd got some proper charts, and then I could use my GPS to confirm exactly where I am. Eventually I could make out land and headed for it. It turns out to be Porth Neigwl, a big surfing bay. As I can't see any lee shores around this will have to do. The surfing waves are quite big, but I made a safe landing, then it's up with the tent which now smells like a wet dog, and has started to leak.

It looks like a long walk to the nearest village, so I'll make do with the emergency supplies. To cap it all I have run out of drinking water. Have you ever had tea made with lemonade? It tastes like lemsip (but cheaper). So that was my first month, and I should be at Barmouth according to my schedule. I am in fact about 10 miles up on the deal, so I'm quite pleased really.

<u>Tuesday June 1st</u>
I bailed out the tent at 2.00, 3.00, and finally got up at 6.00 - I may as well be sailing in it rather than just lying in it!! The good thing is that I can pack everything whilst in the tent so most things stay dry, apart from my sleeping bag which is going to need some drying out if it ever stops raining.
I have found that this sailing lark is a bit like flying, the difficult bit is the take off and landing. Today was no exception, as I try to get through the big breaking waves. It's OK if there is enough wind to launch between waves, and you make some forward progress before being pushed back by the next one. After one or two crashing waves, the well is completely swamped, but if you get past the breakers it's no problem to bail out, as the well is so small. It's almost worthwhile capsizing, though because the boat then comes up dry.
I replaced the self bailer at Bude, but the new one is now not working, as it keeps getting rucked up (yes I said rucked) with all the sand when I beach. I think I will take it off and just put the bung in, and use a half of a plastic bottle to bail out, in calm seas. In rough and windy weather I think it will still self drain to a certain extent. The self bailer is fine if you are using a trolley on the beaches. I set off, and went through Bardsley Sound, past the elusive Bardsley Island that I kept seeing, and then losing yesterday.
Then past Porth Oer, or Whistling Sands, as it is called, because of the sound the sand makes when you walk on it in warm, dry weather. This strange phenomenon is caused by peculiarly shaped particles of fine sand being rubbed together. There was not much chance of me hearing it in the pouring rain though. I was now beating northwards and mindful of the fact that I needed to find Fort Belan, which was built to guard the Menai Straits against a Napoleonic invasion.
Unfortunately I mistook the ruins of the 15th century church, behind the Llanddwyn lighthouse for Fort Belam, and merrily sailed right into Maltraeth Yard, about five miles up the river Cefni, before I realised that I was not in the Menai Straits at all. The trouble is that only at low tide can you see how small the river is, and the rest of the time there is a lagoon like expance of sheltered water.
As it was getting dark by now, I quit for the day, and went to the local pub to confirm that I was where I think I was. Then it was back to put up the

soggy tent, and worse still get into the soggy sleeping bag.

My feet were still cold, and I knew I wouldn't get to sleep without warming them, so out with the hot water bottle, and two minutes later, I was a bit more comfortable. The trouble was that when the bottle goes cold, so do I. the hot water bottle is not able to keep me warm and also dry the sleeping bag as well, as it is so wet. So every two hours I have to re-boil the water. I really must get a new tent - one of those quick erect ones - two strokes and it's up. (not sure about the tent though).

Wednesday June 2nd

I knew that today I would either go through the Menai Straits or go around Anglesey. I know it will take longer to go round, but I am told that going through the Straits is something you shouldn't miss out on, as it is the weirdest feeling - like white water rafting. So I suppose I'll just have to get on with it, and get it over ASAP.

I needed to get to Caernarfon at 2.30 for low tide, so I had a sort of lie in. Fortunately the sun came out so I was able to start to dry my tent, and sleeping bag. A fisherman who lived nearby insisted on giving me a full English, after hearing my potted story so far. It is amazing how kind some people are. I packed all my gear up which was now all dry at last, and popped round the lighthouse and up to Caernarfon by 1.00.

I had an hour and a half to wait so I went to the local newspaper to see if they could print my story, and promote my Charity, but also to take a photo with the Castle as a backdrop which would have looked fantastic. Sadly the photographer was not around so I missed out on the picture, but they did print the story. The castle was built by Edward I in 1282, and in 1301 he proclaimed his eldest son Prince of Wales. 668 years later, Prince Charles was invested with the same title during a similar colourful ceremony held in the courtyard.

I left at about 2.15, which was too early. As I got into the main channel the ebb was still quite fierce, so I was going backwards. I landed and waited for a few minutes. At last I could see it was beginning to slacken, and pushed off once again.

This time it was fine, but as I got further inland, the wind was non existent, but I was going at a rapid rate of knots, and white water rafting was an apt description. I seemed to have little control over the boat, it was just going with the flood. I shot under the railway bridge and then almost immediately under Thomas Telford's 100ft. high suspension bridge, which, when it opened in 1826 was the longest single span in the world. As I came out into Conway Bay, the current eased, and I could see a lot of dinghies sailing up towards Beaumaris. I crept slowly into the jetty, still with little wind.

It was 7.30, and would not be low tide until 8.30. Weird when you think that it was low tide at Caernarfon six hours ago, and it is only about twelve miles away. As I landed I was offered the use of a trolley, and welcomed to The Royal Anglesey Yacht Club. They couldn't offer a bed for the night, but said I could sleep in the dinghy park alongside Oops. There then followed much quaffing of beer, and much collecting of sponsorship money, before locking myself into the dinghy park for the night. A great night and I am very grateful to all of the sailors who sponsored me.

Thursday June 3rd

I let myself out of the dinghy park, and used the trolley to get to the waterline (luxury). The wind felt stronger than the force 4 to 5 that was forecast, but I thought I could handle it. As it was coming from the south west, I would be running with it all day.

As I left Beaumaris, I could see the famous castle, which was built by Edward I in 1295, and is considered the finest example of a concentrically designed fortress in Britain. I had to be careful here as I ran aground on the Lavan Sands which seem to go for miles and I had to gybe to keep close to the Anglesey coast, until I almost got to Black Point, before gybing again and heading for Llanfairfechan. This gybe unfortunately wasn't successful, and I capsized, which is never nice when gybing on a Laser.

The great thing is to stay with the boat, which I always do, as I have a lifeline attached which I religiously attach before setting out each morning. The only trouble is that invariably this line snags on something, and I have to unhook before righting the boat. I was getting fairly tired, (nothing to do with last night's beer) and having only done a few miles, decided to land at Llanfairfechan, take stock of the situation and either reef right down or give up for the day.

Landing proved difficult in the big breaking waves, and I decided to wait for an hour, to see if there was an improvement. I had a gut feeling that going on was not the right thing to do, so after half an hour I pulled Oops up to the high water line, and set about getting some food. I went to a local café and had an industrial sized portion of chicken and chips followed by Treacle pudding and custard. I had a horse once called treacle - he had a golden stirrup. I looked round for a camping shop, but to no avail. The wind was strong all day, and at dusk it started to rain, so I decided to put the tent up in a shelter on the promenade and get an early night.

Friday June 4th

I was woken up by a chap emptying the bins along the front. He had been in the Navy before retiring, and now just does this job for pin money. He was interested in my story, and word gets around, because before I left, I had a visit from the Mayor and a cameraman from the local paper.

The weather was much better than yesterday, and I shot across on a reach to Great Ormes Head, one of Britain's most impressive headlands, 679ft high, where, on a clear day, you can see Snowdonia, The Isle of Man, and The Lake District. Still on a reach, I went past the huge Victorian and Edwardian hotels in Llandudno, the largest Welsh resort. I was really flying now, past Colwyn Bay, Rhyl, and Prestatyn. I had been told to keep to the shore side of a huge wind farm just off the Point of Air, but then head out to sea at the River Dee estuary, as there are some pretty awful sandbanks. I didn't go far enough out, and managed to get stuck a couple of times.

While I was busy figuring out which way to go, I managed to capsize a couple of times, and bent my tiller again at about a 40degree angle. I could see Little Hilbre with West Kirby behind. As I came near to Hoylake, I could see the tide must be out about 3 miles - not a good place to land.

The Wirral's sandbanks have claimed many victims back in the age of sail, and the dunes were too unstable to support a lighthouse. But a ship loaded with cotton ran aground here in 1761 and it's cargo was left to rot on the beach. The combination of sand and salt water turned the bales into a "raft", that was so strong it formed the base for The Leasowe lighthouse. It does seem strange having a lighthouse here, as it's halfway between the estuaries of the Rivers Dee and Mersey.

I was hoping to get into The Mersey - New Brighton will have much less sand at low tide. I eventually got to Wallasey, at 9.45, and decided that it wasn't worth the risk of going further, as the light was fading fast, and there may be lots of traffic in the Mersey estuary, who wouldn't be able to see such a small boat as mine. I pulled Oops up a little way onto the beach, and walked with my waterproof bags up to the high tide line.

As I came back, I could see that Oops was actually following me in as quickly as I could push her on the fender, so I took the mast and sail back to my bags and started putting up the tent. I prepared another gastronomic meal, (spaghetti, bolognese from a tin) always watching that Oops was still on her way, and hadn't decided to go further along the coast. By about 11.30 she was nearly up to high tide mark, albeit a couple of hundred yards away. I walked her back in the water, and just had to drag her up the last few yards - quite a good plan as long as you have the patience to wait for the tide to do all the work, and can keep an eye on the boat.

It had been a good day, and I was now back in England. Wales is the first country I can say I have sailed right round.

CHAPTER 7

WALLASSEY TO PORT LOGAN

<u>Saturday June 5th</u>
I knew it was not worth getting up early today, as the tide would be miles out, so there was no point in attempting to sail until high tide at 12.00. I was therefore on a mission to get a new tent before then.
It was quintessential that I obtained a reasonably priced portable shelter from the egregious, disingenuous scousers, although I knew they would pusillanimously demand lots of the filthy wonga from me. There I've done it. I've managed to get all my friend Chris's favourite words into one sentence.
No luck in Wallasey, or New Brighton, but someone told me there was an Index shop in Birkenhead. Success, a new tent at last, but not a quick erection jobbie - oh well I don't mind doing it slowly.
I phoned Hilary up to wish her "Bon Voyage", as she was going to the mid-west of America today, with Lisa, her niece, to round up and drive unbroken horses for a week, then another week on the beach in Florida. I always said I was going to Tampa with her, but I can't now as she has gone without me.
I got back to the beach and ceremoniously threw my old tent in the bin, and then it was off in light airs towards Blackpool.
I passed the Mersey Estuary, always mindful of the ships coming and going. Past Formby, then up to Southport. The 14,300 acre wildfowl sanctuary here has a tide that goes out four miles which is amazing. I went across the River Ribble and stayed well clear of Lytham St. Anne's, where 13 men of St. Anne's lifeboat, and 14 from Southport's lifeboat lost their lives trying to reach the German Barque *Mexico* in 1886 - the worst disaster in British lifeboat history. At about 9.00 it was getting dark as I approached Blackpool, and I thought it best to land before the South Pier and the Golden Mile where there would be less rumbustious people to contend with overnight.
Today's problem was that the tide had still a long way to go out, before I could use yesterday's trick of letting the tide actually bring Oops in. So I decided to drag her in as I really wanted to get a meal in town, and it would be well after midnight before the tide came right in. It still took about an hour and a half to successfully make my way right up the beach, again with people watching, but no volunteers (it's grim up north).
By 10.30 I was knackered, but at least I was sitting in a pub with a pint in my hand. There was food, and a cabaret act. A guy went from George Formby to Roy Orbison without catching his breath. He was the best I have seen.

Sunday June 6th

Amazingly we were here in Blackpool on exactly the same day two years ago when we cycled round Britain's coastline.

Another lie in as again it would be after lunch before I could easily set sail. I decided to go for a walk/jog to take my mind off sailing. I seem to have been eating, drinking, and breathing sailing, for a long time, and I need to unwind a bit. I then found a decent café, where I had a huge three course Sunday lunch, with all the trimmings for £3.50. Brilliant!

I set off in very calm conditions, drifting past the Blackpool Tower, and all the funfair rides, then past Cleveleys, and on to Fleetwood. I knew that if I didn't get right onto the edge of the River Wyre, I would be in trouble with the sandbanks at low tide. This is serious stuff around here - The Saltings of the Wyre-Lune Sanctuary stretch for six miles.

I made it near to the Knott-End ferry landing stage, where I dragged Oops up the steep riverbank. I knew I wouldn't have trouble getting off tomorrow morning.

Not many miles done today, but at least I could start early tomorrow, and hopefully have all day to get past the horrendous sand banks of Morecambe Bay. As the tide was ebbing I could see that there is only a very small channel by which to leave tomorrow, and I will have to be well out to sea all day.

Monday June 7th

I was up bright and early to get the ebbing tide across Morecambe Bay to Barrow. The visibility was poor, but a south westerly force 3 to 4 was OK. The channel out of the Wyre was well marked, and a few big fishing boats were a comfort.

However soon I lost site of land behind and once again my compass was my only friend. I could see a ship coming out from Sunderland, so I knew I was past the River Lune Estuary. My bearing should be about nor-nor west, but when you can't see anything you always tend to err on the safety (land) side. After a couple of hours I could vaguely see a shape to the west, so I knew I had gone too far northwards. At the same time the centreboard hit the bottom, and I assumed that I hadn't completely avoided Morecambe Bay. I headed south west assuming the shape I could see was The Isle of Walney. It turned out to be Foulney Island, as I could soon see the Walney Nature Reserve behind.

Once round the end of Walney, it was back to a north westerly course, and a relief to see the industrial area that could only be Barrow-in-Furness, which once had the world's biggest ironworks. I wasn't out of the metaphoric woods yet though, I could either land here with the big tides or go further

north past Duddon Sands. I landed and ran for ten minutes or so to try and get some warmth back in my hands and feet.
I knew someone who tried to keep warm in a canoe, by lighting a fire. Needless to say the canoe went up in smoke, which just goes to show "you can't have your kayak and heat it too".
A quick bite to eat, then I decided that I would do better to push on and get past the sand, sand, and more sand that has been plaguing me for days. It would be ok if the tide times were in my favour, but I always seem to want to stop sailing when it's low tide, and start sailing again next day when it's low tide. I headed out to sea again, and got round The Duddon Estuary, past Haverigg, and along the coast where I could see the sand was turning to shingle, and becoming rockier, so I knew the drag up the beach would be easier from now onwards.
I was again getting cold and decided to call it a day, near a grassy bank, which looked like a suitable camping spot. I knew I was near Ravensglas, but I was tired and happy just to stay here without searching for a pub. It wasn't that simple though because I ended up walking for what seemed like miles to get a signal on the phone. One day I guess we'll be able to get a signal from everywhere - I can't wait.

Tuesday June 8th
I awoke at 5.00 and knew that it would be a good day, with a decent force 3 or 4 behind me. I got prepared, but still like to listen to the shipping forecast at 5.45, in case they have something nasty lined up for later.
All seemed well for the day though, and it was easy sailing, up past the industrial towns of Whitehaven, Workington, and Maryport, where I stopped for food and water which I had run out of again. I must make sure I am stocked up when I am in the wilds' of Scotland. This town derived its name from Mary Senhouse, the wife of a local landowner, who started developing the area in the 18th century. It's hard to imagine that once the docks handled millions of tons of cargo a year before it silted up. Now there are only a few fishing boats, and private craft.
It was decision time again, do I hug the coast, or head across the Solway Firth to Bonny Scotland. Wot the hell - in for a penny! If I keep my eyes on the compass facing north, I can't miss, and as I got nearer to the Scottish Coast, I was able to veer north westerly to get as far westward as I could before landing. I landed in a superb sheltered bay, and having walked up to the main street, discovered it was Rockcliffe, miles further than I had hoped for.
There wasn't much there in the way of shops or pubs, but what a beautiful village and fantastic scenery. I was told that there were a couple of pubs, and

a sailing club just up the road at Kippford. I didn't like to sail further up the estuary against the tide, and thought the club may be closed anyway, so I changed and took my washing tackle with me, and walked/jogged to Kippford where a club member working on his boat let me in to the club for a shower.
I am having problems now with sand under my fingernails, and I put tons of Vaseline on after a shower, which then dries up within minutes. I then went to The Anchor for a couple of pints of "Solway Mist - naturally cloudy". It looked like the stuff I used to make, but tasted much better. Then it was a Chicken Tikka. The landlady and some locals donated some money to Charity - Thanks guys. Then it was back to Rockcliffe where I pitched the tent on the soft sand at 10.30.

Wednesday June 9th
Up early again, so off I went at about 6.00 to get the ebb westwards. I hugged the coast until the bottom of Ross Bay, where I went round Meikle Ross, then headed north westwards across Wigtown Bay towards Garlieston, until I could make out the coastline, then headed south west towards The Isle of Whithorn.
I capsized on the way, as the wind was freshening, and I thought about landing. As I got near to Burrow Head, I realised I had missed the entrance to the harbour so I decided to carry on round to Port William. I should have gone back, because as I got nearer to the headland, the waves were a frightening size, and it was about a mile before they eased back to something sensible. The large swells are OK, as the laser can climb up and over them, but if they are too small, she nosedives and submerges the bows and all the bags as well. I was then on a good reach north westwards up the coast to Port William, where I managed to capsize just outside the harbour entrance. It was only a quick leg over and up again, so I think I got away without anyone spotting it. It was a brilliant day.
What's the difference between an egg, and a good day on a Laser? - You can beat an egg, but you can't beat a good day on a laser. I managed to find a Library, and sent off some E-mails.
I had a meal in the Clansman, where Brian, the Landlord insisted on paying for my meal, and phoned Louise from The Galloway Gazette, and George from the Lifeboat Station, who both came round for a photo-shoot on the slipway in the harbour. We had a good night in The Clansman, and I went to bed sozzled again, after putting the tent up on the slipway next to Oops.

Thursday June 10th

I woke early and tried to repair the mast hole again with filler, but when I filled it up with water later on in the day, it was still leaking like a sieve. I couldn't see the end of the harbour wall for the fog, so there was no way that I was going out in that. I took the tent down anyway, hoping that I would be able to leave later in the day.

The mist didn't really lift all day, which was a shame because there was quite a good wind blowing. I was told that it would be better to go straight across the south of Luce Bay to Maryport, if the visibility is better tomorrow, as the Army have been busy blowing up dummy mines in the middle of the bay. Apparently the fishermen have been out in the bay crossing out "MINE" and painting "YOURS" on them all.

It was a good day in the Clansman, everyone has been kind with some more money collected for charity, and an interview with the local radio station. Pam, one of Brian's friends let me use her computer to send out more emails. I then managed to do some washing in the gents loos.

There is a life sized statue of a man leaning on a rail, looking out to sea near the harbour, and wherever you go your eyes are drawn to it - Is it real or is it the statue - weird.

I tested the mast hole again - still no good - so this time I managed to get some fibre glass resin, and matting from George, who also runs the hardware shop. Hopefully this will work for now. It's a bad design, as the mast is grinding away with no bearing surface, all day long. Mind you I am doing more sailing in a month than most laser sailors do in ten years, assuming you do only a couple of one and a half hour races per week during the summer.

I had another session in the Clansman in the evening, then early to bed, after putting the tent up on the slipway again, as I wanted to be away early next morning.

Friday June 11th

I left at about 7.00 to get the ebbing tide which is strong westward in the Solway Firth. My plan was to make sure I got round The Mull Of Galloway (the most Southerly point in Scotland) before the tide turned and flooded back up the Firth.

The wind was against me all the way across Luce Bay, but at least the current was dragging me westwards. It was about 1.00 before I first spotted the Lighthouse, and then reached The Mull, but once again the huge seas were a nightmare. As I rounded the headland, a breaking wave crashed over the bows, slewing Oops around, wrenching the mainsheet from my hand, and for a while the only contact I had was my toes under the strap, and my hand on the tiller extension. Fortunately as the sail was now loose, I avoided a capsize, and I was soon back in contact.

The last confrontation between the Picts and the Scots was supposed to have occurred here and the last living Pict jumped to his doom from The Mull, clutching the recipe for heather beer. I could have done with a few pints of it myself in the next few hours, as the tide turned and the wind died, leaving me to slop about in the big waves but making no headway.

There was no safe place to land, and it wasn't until the tide turned again that I started going north again. I eventually made Port Logan at 9.30, fourteen and a half hours after leaving Port William, and only managed about 25 miles in all that time.

I was cold, wet, had a sore bum, and shattered. I managed to change on the beach and rush to the pub, but too late for food. I settled for a couple of beers, phoned the Coastguard, and Guy, who is my land-based contact while Hilary is away doing desperate things with horses. Then back to put up the tent in the dark. A hot water bottle then - you've guessed it, a tinned all day breakfast - the first hot thing since my early morning tea, seventeen hours ago.

CHAPTER 8

PORT LOGAN TO LOCH STORNAWAY

Saturday June 12th
I slept well last night, not surprisingly really. When we cycled here they were filming *1000 Miles of Sky*, but now it is all back to how it should be - it looks better now.
I phoned the Coastguard up to let him know I was going northwards, but he was reluctant to let me go. I had missed the shipping forecast, and he told me that it will get quite windy later. OK so I'll land if it gets bad, it can't be worse than yesterday round The Mull. I assured him I'd be careful, and prepared to leave. Within about ten minutes a Coastguard Landrover appeared, and two further guys tried to persuade me to stay put. I tried to reason with them, and they agreed that they couldn't stop me and it was my decision, so off I went. By now I was well into the ebb, and made good progress with the tide but against the wind.
By lunchtime, the tide turned, and I was struggling to make headway, so I decided to land at Portpatrick.
Outside the harbour there were a couple of yachts head up to wind, taking their sails down, and preparing to motor into the swell at the harbour entrance. I had no choice but to shoot through the swell, under full sail, then worry about the landing once in the relative calm of the harbour. I checked out the northern part of the harbour, but there were only moorings with about 8 yachts and a few fishing boats. To the south there was a small sandy beach, which looked as though it would still be there at high tide, so I dragged Oops onto the nice soft sand. I felt like an outcast, me at one end, and every one else at the other.
By the time I had struggled out of my wet suit and walked to the pub, the other yachts that I saw outside the harbour were still faffing about trying to moor up. It turned out that all the yachts were from the Ulster Yacht Club, on a weekend away. A great drinking lunch was soon under way, followed by a charity collection, when they got wind of why I was sailing a Laser in fairly inhospitable waters. They raised lots of money.
It looked as though they would be at it all afternoon, but I had a few jobs to do on Oops, so back to the beach and over with the boat, and much filling of holes, when who should look down from the car park but Peter Barr, my old work colleague. He moved to the Galloway Peninsular some time ago, and just happened to have booked a table at the restaurant that I will be sleeping ten yards from tonight. Oh well, perhaps one more pint then,

followed by an excellent meal, as they managed to squeeze another chair at the table. As Peter and his party left about 9.00, I decided to have an early night, and put the tent up.

Some local kids were curious about why the boat was there and why I was sleeping on the beach, and wanted a blow by blow account of my journey so far. I excused myself and went to bed in a semi drunken stupor, leaving them to their games on the beach.

Sunday June 13th

I woke up for the shipping forecast as usual, and as I undid the tent, I could see lots of flowers had been planted all around the tent, and good luck messages on scraps of paper and also written in the sand. I assumed it was the kids - what a nice gesture - until a couple, who owned the flowers came down and went absolutely ballistic, thinking I had pinched them. Once I explained, they calmed down and even offered me breakfast, which I declined. Fortunately the flowers were still attached to the roots, and the couple were soon busy re-planting them in their rightful place.

Meanwhile I was packing up everything, and discovered that my fender, (which was now at the other end of the beach) had been burst. I assumed the kids had been responsible, so I quickly went round to the Harbour Master, who very kindly let me have an old one that was kicking about in his shed. He even lent me his bike to get back to Oops, saying he would collect the bike later, knowing that I wanted to get as much of the ebbing tide as possible - some people are so kind.

There was a good force 3 to 4 blowing from behind so I was making good progress past Corsewell Point, Loch Ryan, Ballantrae, Girvan, and Turnberry Castle, which was the childhood home of Robert the Bruce. All along the coast here can be seen the amazing Aisla Craig, a volcanic pyramid of rock, ten miles off the coast of Girvan. Granite quarries produce curling stones, and it is a major bird breeding station for gannets, kittiwakes, guillemot and razorbills. After passing Maidens I was slowing down, as the wind died, so I decided to stop for the night right next to the magnificent Culzean Castle.

We were here two years ago, so I knew that there was a camp site actually in the grounds of the castle, albeit a good half hour's walk from my landing point. I changed and began the walk through the well groomed grounds, and when I got to the camp site, I explained about my charity adventure and why I couldn't actually camp here, but would it be OK for me to use the shower, which I was of course willing to pay for. The manager said that I could only have a shower if I paid the stopover fee of £4.70. I thought this a bit steep especially as I am a Member of The Camping and Caravanning Club who he works for. I also explained that I had an excellent shower at Portpatrick Harbour for 20p. Mr. Jobsworth wasn't going to budge, so I bade him farewell, and promised to give the £4.70 to charity - some people are so UNkind.

I walked back to Maidens, and had a meal, but couldn't get any bread from the pub. I got chatting to a couple who used to live in Eastbourne, who let me have half a loaf, and wouldn't take any money for it.

Then it was back three miles to the boat, and another pleasant night on a sandy beach.

Monday June 14th

The forecast was not good, force 5 to 6. But worse the mist was really thick - I couldn't see the end of the bay, so I decided to stay put for the day. My plan was to head westward, south of Arran, and try for The Mull of Kintyre, so there was no point in struggling further up the coast in the mist, and then if the weather is fine tomorrow, head southwards.

I had a lie in, but was woken about 8.00 by a Scottish National Trust official, who told me I wasn't allowed to camp on their land. I said I thought the entire coastline was owned by The Queen, and she said I could. Apparently that is true of most coastline, (not about her telling me I could) but when the Scottish National Trust buy the land they always buy right down to the low water line. Anyway I explained why I was there, and he was happy for my boat to be there, so I said I would take the tent down, and put it up after he had gone home for the night. As long as I got it down before he comes tomorrow, he wouldn't know, so all would be Hunky Dory.

I had a pleasant day in the mist, looking round Culzean Castle, which was built in 1777 by Robert Adam for the Earl of Cassillis. It is a magnificent mixture of Gothic exuberance, and Georgian elegance. The grounds form Scotland's first Country Park. There are Magnolias, Monterey cypresses, Chinese palms and Chilean myrtles, to name but a few. On the lake, there were many ducks, and I had the unpleasant experience of seeing some gulls swooping down and taking ducklings from under their mums noses (or should that be beaks) a horrible sight!

Tuesday June 15th

I didn't quite get the tent down in time, but I promised to be away by 10.00. There was a westerly wind blowing, so I was beating across north westwards towards the bottom of Arran.

On the way a fantastic square rigger called Jeannie (something) from Tralee, was on a converging course with me. I shouted up to the crew, explained what I was doing, and they threw some lunch down to me in a plastic bag, before they disappeared up The Firth of Clyde, and I headed south west towards The Mull of Kintyre.

There were more gannets than usual today. They have a six foot wingspan, and work individually dropping like a stone from fifty feet into the sea, and pop up two seconds later sometimes with, and sometimes without a fish. They also operate in squadrons of twenty or so, in precise formation - they all stop flapping and glide for about one hundred yards, then all flap again in unison - it's just like watching the Red Arrows. I spotted one asleep on the water, curled up like a ball, with head and feet tucked in. I got to about three feet of it before it sensed me, then all hell broke loose - one squawk, everything unravelled and it took off like a Harrier Jump Jet - fantastic. Mind you these birds are small compared to the Royal Albatrosses that we saw in New Zealand - they have an incredible eleven feet wingspan, and spend about eight days and 11,000 miles at sea as they go round the world collecting food, whilst the other one of the pair baby sits. Then it's all change and the other one is off for eight days.

I could see Sanda Island clearly to the south of Southend, where I was heading for, and knew that there were nice sandy bays, with a campsite on one of them. It is also on a lee shore so I was not too worried about the landing. It still took a long time to get there, and I didn't land until about 7.30.

It had been a great day. My cunning plan to go straight across under Arran paid off, and I made up five days on my original schedule. It was nice to have a shower straight away, put the tent up, and not worry about potential vandals - you feel that much safer on a camp site. I found a pub about half a mile away, and met an Aussie there. You learn something every day - I asked him why we are called POME's and he said it is because when we used to deport people to Australia, they had to wear overalls with **P**risoner **O**f **M**other **E**ngland written on the back. It seems cockeyed to me, I think in that case it is them that should be POME's. He also said that at a recent cabaret show he was at, a comedian asked "Are there any Aussies in tonight". He said "Yes". Then the comedian said "Welcome back to the scene of the crime".

Wednesday June 16th

Very little wind today, but as I set sail I could see Ireland as clear as a bell. I was so tempted just to hop over and back, just to say I had been to Ireland as well on this trip. However, I had no maps and the wind wasn't strong enough so I kept my sensible head on and just drifted round the Mull Of Kintyre on the tide. It took ages making any headway, and when I got to Macrihanish, I called it a day.

I am still using Germoline, and Vaseline on my sore bits, but now my behind is sore and uncomfortable, and as some people think the sun shines from that general direction I think I must be developing Polaroids!! I went to the doctor and said I have a problem with my bowels. He asked if I was regular, and I said "Oh yes as regular as clockwork, every morning at 7.00. My trouble is that I don't get up until 8.00".

Thursday June 17th
I was up unexpectedly early at 2.00 as Oops was trying to get in the tent with me. I jumped out stark naked (except for socks), moved the tent and then Oops further up the beach in the pouring rain. Then it was back to the tent, with an open door, and the rain lashing in. A hot water bottle was called for before trying for more sleep. Life can be pleasant at times!!!
I dozed most of the morning between and during heavy downpours, as there was no chance of sailing today for me.
At lunchtime the landlady at the pub very kindly added a loaf of bread to her shopping list for me, when she went to the local shop in Campbeltown - 7 miles away.
A notice in the village read - At the Chapel of Cille Coivin, in the 13th century St. Kevin inaugurated the custom for unhappily married couples to gather together annually and run blindfolded round the chapel three times. On a command they stop and grab the nearest member of the opposite sex, to whom they are "married" for the next 12 months. If they are still dissatisfied they can keep returning. If I'd been around then, it would be just my luck to keep getting the same bloody one!!! Back to the pub in the evening and later on armed with my loaf of bread for an early night, now with the tent hopefully well above the high tide line.

Friday June 18th
The forecast was for a northerly 3 to 4, which was better than yesterday, but it still meant tacking all day. I left at 8.00 and made some good progress, past Glenbarr, and through the Sound of Gigha.
The scenery was getting rugged and desolate here and the wind was getting stronger as I reached Ardpatrick Point. There were some pretty big white horses now so I hugged the shore, and popped into Loch Stornaway. I capsized and decided that to land on the lee shore was the safest bet on the northern end of the Loch. I spotted a 50 foot beach of pure white sand, with a turquoise sea just in front. It could have been in The Caribbean, if it wasn't so bloody cold. I quickly pulled Oops up onto the beach, got dry and changed. I could see on my map that there was a road close by, but I couldn't see it from my little bay. I climbed up through the ferns onto the road, and

met Murray and his wife, who were returning from a walk to their car. Murray offered me a lift to the campsite, just past Kilberry, where I had a shower and a curry. Then it was back to my little beach, it's amazing how warm you feel once you are dry and well fed.

Once back on the beach, I realised what an amazing place this is. I can see Gigha, Islay, Jura, and Mull from here. Jura is the closest and also the most impressive with the Paps standing tall and proud - 3 peaks between 2400 and 2600 feet high. I feel just like Robinson Crusoe, on his desert island. By the way did you know he's leaving Friday?

CHAPTER 9

LOCH STORNAWAY TO ISLE OF SKYE

<u>Saturday June 19th</u>
I think the curry I had last night must have been prehistoric - I certainly woke up with a megasaurarse.
I am now half way round Britain, but I can't go anywhere today, as the wind is much too strong. It's strange, that now I am well into this sailing lark, I have developed a sixth sense for knowing when I can or can't sail. (Or as I like to call it - a gut feeling) Often the forecast is quite good for the area I am in, but I just know that in reality it's quite different. Also just listening to the forecast for all other areas builds up a picture in my mind about whether to sail or not.
Still if you are stuck somewhere, where better than here. I have always dreamed of sailing around the Scottish Isles on a big yacht, but now I can see the advantage of doing it in a dinghy. To be stuck on a beach like this when the weather claggs in, is far better than to be stuck in one of the smelly harbours, or stuck in a bay at anchor, being tossed about all the time.
I have formulated a few ideas to make Oops more comfortable for cruising/camping, and when I get back home, my next project will be to try for a prototype that will fit the bill for cruising round the Scottish Isles. The trouble is that most dinghies are either out and out racers, or else if they are designed to "cruise" they are too heavy to drag up onto a beach. A sailing boat, for all its complexity, is in fact a version of simplicity, but in a complex way. I have known engineers who just can't get the hang of sailing, but if you have ever looked inside, say, a gearbox of a modern car - how can you possibly begin to understand its workings? These same engineers would see it as a doddle. Anyway, watch this space to see if my design ever works.

<u>Sunday June 20th</u>
The forecast was still not good, with another fresh northerly wind blowing. My gut feeling said I would be OK if I hugged the coast. I was still on the lee shore, so the wind wasn't strong here, but I put a reef in the sail, knowing it would be blowing once out of Loch Stornaway.
As I came out of the Loch, I thought I would have to land as soon as possible to put another reef in, so I headed for the first decent beach which was next to the campsite. As I came in to land, the wind was easing so much that I actually took the reef out, and in fact I was under full sail all day - so much for the forecast. I have to be careful that I look far enough ahead to avoid

just going up into the big Lochs, that are so wide at their entrance. I only just spotted the Point of Knap and headed for it, otherwise I would have gone right up Loch Caolisport, and wasted a lot of time. The same happened at Loch Sween. As I went northwards past Tayvallich, the sea seemed to be bubbling and strange ripples appeared, and I realised that I was amongst the whirlpools that occur here.

I don't know which way to wiggle the tiller, but fortunately there was enough wind to drag me through. I landed on a tiny beach in Loch Crinan for a warm up run. I should be used to the cold, as our house was freezing when I was a kid, although my dad used to boast that we were the first to have central heating. We used to have a candle on the table that we would all huddle round, and if it got really cold, sometimes he would light it.

After my run, I looked around and I could see the end of the famous Crinan Canal, which was opened in 1801. It is only eight and a half miles long, but saves the 130 mile sea journey round the Kintyre peninsular. Here I could also see the 12th century Duntrune Castle. The views are spectacular, but I must press on. As I sail north westwards, I could soon see the open sea as I round the north of Jura, and have to decide whether to go to the east or west of Luing. I decided that I would prefer to be on the more open west side, so I can avoid all the tiny islands, and get a feel for a decent landing, if I can't get as far as Mull. A few months ago I would almost certainly have opted for the most sheltered (East) option. I thought that Cullipool would be a good place to stop, but I felt it was a bit exposed, and carried on right up to Easdale, where I landed on a really sheltered lee shore.

Another excellent day, with some absolutely breathtaking scenery, as good if not better than The Bay of Islands in New Zealand that we visited in February this year. I certainly intend to spend many holidays in this neck of the woods. The only downfall is that it is so bloody cold, but perhaps when this northerly wind changes, it will warm up – it's nearly midsummer for god's sake. I went to a local village dance in the evening which was great fun, and they had the usual spot prizes, - a hot pot, a tea pot, and a pistol.

<u>Monday June 21st</u>
I had a lie in this morning. I managed to fall asleep after the shipping forecast, and didn't wake up until 9.00. I went for a wash in the public loos, all of which are excellent in Scotland, with hot water, toilet rolls, but still normally without plugs for the sinks. I'm sure they are built with plugs, but they always disappear within days.

I spoke to the man who operates a ferry to the small island to the west. I asked if he could give me any information about the tides in The Sound of Mull, as I was intending to go through to Tobermory today. He said he only ever goes the 500 yards to the island and back, so he couldn't help. He did tell me that like me he phones the Coastguard to let them know when he's working, and they always try to give him the traffic news for the whole of Scotland. He only runs a foot passenger service.

I set off in light winds and took five hours to reach Duart Castle, although I could see it in the distance for ages. This castle is on the south east headland of Mull, and has been the home of The Maclean Clan for 700 years. The English occupied it after Bonnie Prince Charlie's troops were crushed in 1746, and later fell into disrepair, but was restored in 1912. As I rounded the headland, the wind picked up, but I had to beat all the way up the Sound of Mull, stopping a few times for a warm up run. I reached Tobermory at 10.00, but there are no beaches at high tide. To the east, I spotted the Caledonian MacBrayne (known in this neck of the woods as Calmac) ferry slipway, and decided that would do. I pulled Oops up and "parked" her in the first car parking bay. This was not an ideal place, as I was locked in the Calmac compound. Fortunately once I had changed, I only had to hop over the gate, and I was at the end of the "High Street". I was too late for food in the pub, but I spotted an Indian Restaurant at 10.55, that would shut at 11.00. They took pity on me and I had a really nice curry - fortunately not a prehistoric one this time. Then it was back to the boat, and up with the tent in the next parking bay.

Tuesday June 22nd
I was awake as usual for the shipping forecast, which was not good with very little wind. I got dressed and took the tent down, because I didn't want any officials to know that I stayed the night on their property, and was slightly embarrassed about being there.

I decided to explore this lovely little town, well - village really. It was founded in 1788, when the British Fisheries Society decided to take advantage of its sheltered natural harbour. 200 years before, the *Duque di Florencia*, a Spanish Galleon took shelter in the bay. She was thought to be one of the Armada's treasure ships, with 3 million gold doubloons aboard. She was sunk by Donald Maclean, who managed to ignite the gunpowder store. There has been lots of salvage attempts, and many relics found, but it is believed that the bulk of the treasure is still buried at the bottom of the bay. The name Tobermory is derived from the Gaelic Tobar Mhoire, which means St. Mary's well. The well can still be seen on the outskirts of the town. To the north of Tobermory is Bloody Bay, whose name is derived from the battle that took place here in 1439, when the Macleans joined forces with the Lord of the Isles - ruler of all the western isles - to defeat his rebel son. However, enough of the History lesson, and back to sailing. I sneaked back into the compound, and waited until the next ferry departed, before quickly getting changed into my wet suit, loading up, dragging the boat to the water's edge, setting sail, and away before many more cars arrived. As I got around the headland, another ferry was approaching, so I was lucky not to get into an embarrassing situation on the slipway. It was painfully slow across to the Point of Ardnamurchan, which is the most westerly point on mainland Britain. Once round the point, I drifted slowly past Sanna Bay, and about two miles later I stopped completely, with nowhere to land. I figured that I was about half way between Sanna and Kilmory, which looked like the next decent place to land, so I decided to paddle to Kilmory. (Always forward if possible).

It took about another two hours to reach this small bay, and after landing, I actually fell asleep in the sun, on the soft grassy bank just above the beach - bliss. I then set off to get a signal on the old mobile, but failed miserably, so I went back to the beach, and spotted a house about 200 yards away. They let me use their phone, and also gave me half a loaf of bread. I asked the Coastguard how you spell "wind" He said "W.I.N.D." So I said what about the 'F'. and he said "There's no 'F' in wind".....

Wednesday June 23rd

I awoke to pouring rain and high winds, so no sailing today. It is amazing the contrast between today and yesterday. I decided to walk to Kilchoan, which is a good five miles away, but I needed to buy some groceries, so off I set. After about half a mile, the person who let me use his phone yesterday, appeared in his car, and gave me a lift there.

I found a Community Centre where I was able to get a shower. I had a serious look at my hands and feet which now look like four raw bits of meat, and it doesn't seem to make a difference how much Vaseline I put on. I did some emails, and had some lunch. Then it was across to the shop and a walk back to the tent in the pouring rain. Someone once wrote that true happiness can be sought, thought, or caught, but never bought. Wise words, mate, wise words. I'll reflect on that the next time I'm bailing out in a force eight.

Thursday June 24th

The weather forecast still sounds bad, but better than yesterday, so I put in a reef and set off. I started off ok, but a little bit overpowered, and I was beginning to get tired, so I landed on another pure white beach, near Loch Moidart, went for a warm up run, and then put in another reef.

It's amazing how effective a reef is. A reef is like valium for boats - it stops them being hyperactive. I managed to cross the Sound of Arisaig, and got into Malaig Harbour, just as the wind was getting even stronger. I found what looked like the only slipway at the back of the harbour, and a nice chap gave me a hand up with the boat. He runs excursions around here, on his fishing boat - and his web site is www.road-to-the-isles.org.uk. I went into town and saw England in the World Cup football match and then the Tennis at Wimbledon on TV. What a disaster…… I understand Henman and Becks are going to train together. Henman will teach Becks how to hit the net and Becks will teach Henman how to miss it.

Friday June 25th
A parcel containing my new VHF radio was waiting for me at the Post Office, and on the way there I spotted a Woolworths - at last some sweets other than Mars Bars - Pick-n-mixtastic.
Before leaving I needed to speak to the locals, as I was about to go through the famous Kyle Rhea, which is a bit like the Menai Straits. If you try to go through against the tide, you ain't gonna make it. I spoke to a fisherman mending his nets, and he told me the best times to go through. He said he left it too late one day, trying to get back home to Malaig, got half way through, and had to crank the engine up to ten knots, but was still going backwards. He didn't get home that night. I left at about midday, but knew that I may be too late to go through this evening, unless the wind stays quite strong.
I started off quite well, past Loch Nevis, and into the Sound of Sleat, with Skye on my left, and the mainland on my right - what fantastic scenery. At about 7.00 the wind was dying, but I was still being pulled northwards by the current. By about 9.30 I could feel the current fading, and knew that I wasn't going to make it through that night. I spotted a reasonable beach in Glenelg Bay, on Skye, and landed without any problems. I would have to wait for the flood tomorrow, but I must be through before 10.00, or I'd be stuck this side again.
It was a lovely little beach, but I am into serious midge country now. I'm told that Avon's "Skin so Soft" is the best remedy, but the only problem is that it makes you smell like a poof. Apparently today has the latest sunset in the year, although the 21st June is the longest day. It's all to do with the curvature of the earth, or the angle of the dangle, or some such technical reason that is beyond me.

CHAPTER 10

ISLE OF SKYE TO DURNESS

Saturday June 26th
It was a quiet night until about 5.00 when the wind got up, and the shipping forecast was pretty bleak with winds getting stronger during the day.
I decided to set sail and see what happens - at least I will be close to the shore on both sides until after Kyle of Lochalsh. I left by 8.00, so I knew I had the tide with me for about two hours. I shot through Kyle Rhea which is only about three miles long, but I managed to have the wind in nearly all points of the compass in that time. The wind was really getting strong, and I decided to land on a lee shore in Loch Alsh, and put in two reefs. This made Oops more manageable, but as I got closer to Kyleakin, I could see that the waves were getting bigger as I got nearer the new bridge, and then the open sea. I decided that my sensible head should be employed, and beached Oops just past the small harbour in Kyleakin. Not a good day, as I have only managed about five miles, but at least I am near civilisation. As I was hauling up, I noticed a 35 to 40 foot yacht was having difficulty getting into the harbour, and eventually gave up, and dropped his anchor about 100 yards from where I was in what was now quite a nasty swell. I changed and went into a bar close to where my boat was, and watched as the people on the big yacht tried to come ashore in their dinghy. They gave up just as I got my second pint (smug bastard). It rained and was windy for the rest of the day, but at least there was plenty of footy on the TV.
I got to bed at about 9.30 as I wanted to get an early start if the weather improves overnight.

Sunday June 27th
I had quite a noisy night, with the wind howling. It calmed down at about 5.00 and the forecast was quite good, with the wind right behind me for a change. I left about 7.00 and once past the new bridge that links Skye to the mainland, I realised that I was on my own, big time.
Across the entrance of Loch Carron, through Caolas Mor, and past Applecross, which is about the most remote village on the mainland. I only saw one other vessel that day, and that was a huge Navel ship, heading for Cape Wrath, where the Nato exercise was happening. The sky was getting darker all the time and by lunch time it was pouring again. Still I'm wet anyway so what's a bit more water? I'm really making up time now, because I am now confident enough to cut right across the entrances of all the Lochs

that I had assumed I would have to go right into. Three of these were Loch Torridon, Loch Gairloch, and Loch Ewe.
Half a dozen dolphins sneaked up and scared me again, as they came so close before leaping out of the water to let me know they were there. Then as I rounded Greenstone Point, I could see Gruinard Island, where to land was prohibited, because it was contaminated by Anthrax during Germ Warfare experiments in the Second World War. So I kept well clear of this and headed for Cailleach Head, and on to Loch Broom, and Ullapool, where I knew there was a campsite right on the water's edge.
I didn't get there until 7.00 - a full 12 hours sailing, but it was great to just pull Oops up and go straight into the shower in the wet suit and gradually thaw out whilst undressing, and showering at the same time.
It had been a great day, but I'm certainly feeling apprehensive about being so alone for such long periods, without even the comfort of the odd fishing boat on the horizon. Still after a good meal, and a couple of pints of "Old Tosser" (something to do with a Caber, not Bush), it was back to the Already erected tent and a comfortable night in a proper campsite.

Monday June 28th
The wind died in the night and the forecast was for a calm day, so I had another good lie in to recover from yesterday's efforts. Then I had a good look at the map, and a chat to the locals. Apparently the Nato exercise doesn't finish until July 1st, and you can't go round Cape Wrath during daylight until after they have finished. I went food shopping, then had an inspection of Oops's bottom and did a few repairs.
A Dutch couple in a camper van next to me was interested in my story, gave me some coffee, and before long a party was in progress, as other campers from various countries including a few Brits came over with cups and cakes. By the time I left at 2.00 there were about 30 people on the shore to wave me off. I felt a bit of a fraud drifting away in virtually no wind - it doesn't seem such an intrepid thing to be doing in such light airs. I only managed to get just past Isle Martin, then to the east of The Summer Isles, where I seemed to be going backwards, so I landed just below a small village called Polglass. I walked to a brand new Community Centre, which was open, but there was no one around. A sign said put 50p in an envelope and leave it in the office, if you want a shower. I can't see that happening in Eastbourne.
So after a shower I popped into the pub, where I met Bill and Linda, who had just retired, and sail an RS400. They were travelling round the country racing at open meetings. Bill's sister belongs to the Pentland Firth Sailing Club, so I took her email address which might come in handy when I get as far as Thurso. A local said "Umm - sailing isn't that where you stand under

a cold shower ripping up fivers?". He's got a point. Still I again collected some Charity money, and yet another mini party was under way, until we were kicked out at closing time.
The great thing about being here at this time of year is that you can put up a tent even at midnight without a torch - it never really gets dark - well perhaps it does at 1o'clock or so but I've never been awake then to see the darkness - if you know what I mean (can you see darkness?).

Tuesday June 29th
The forecast is not good - force 3 to 4, rising to force 6 to 7. So I must stick close to the shore and be prepared to beach.
When I phone the Coastguard, they always ask what the name of the craft is. You would have thought "a Laser Dinghy" would be good enough. How many do they get for gods sake? Anyway I am now in the habit of rattling off "Good morning. This is Ron Pattenden sailing a Laser dinghy named Oops, - that's oscar, oscar, papa, sierra". That seems to keep them happy. Some of them seem to know who I am, and some ask "how many people are there aboard?" I then go on tell them where I am and what my destination is. I pick a time out of thin air for my ETA, which all seems a bit daft really - I don't think I have ever got the ETA correct, and even the destination has only been right a few times. Still at least they know in which direction I'm going.
So off I set with much trepidation about the potential high winds, only to sit about in a force 1 or 2 all day. It is quite sad really as I left the Summer Isles behind, I knew that is the last of all the wonderful islands I have been seeing up the west coast, and there are only Harris and Lewis left which are too far away to be seen anyway.
More Dolphins came to investigate, and the number of puffins floating about was unbelievable - literally thousands. I drifted past a finger of rock called The Old Man of Stoer - quite a site, then past The Point of Stoer, and headed north east to Scourie Bay, where I knew there was another campsite. Scourie Bay is very sheltered and I drifted in just below the campsite. I lugged all my gear onto the first camping terrace, and went to reception to pay. The owner couldn't understand where I had come from - he only ever gets people coming through the front gate. So straight into the shower, again in full gear, and a warm up whilst undressing - bliss. I spent the evening in the local where I met Ben and Phil - two really camp Scotsmen - their surnames were Doone, and McCavity.

Wednesday June 30th
I am getting some conflicting information about the Nato Exercise - does it finish <u>on</u> the first or <u>by</u> the first? The Coastguard seems to think I can't go

round Cape Wrath until the 2nd July, but they can't get anything out of the Navy.

I have decided to stay put in Scourie for the day, and find out from as many sources as possible what the tides are like, should I stay close in or keep well out etc. A chap on the campsite had a pretty tasty looking canoe, so I thought he may know a bit about this neck of the woods. He is involved with an outdoor pursuit centre on Lewis, and gave me a couple of phone numbers to ring.

By the afternoon I was armed with all the information I needed to get round Cape Wrath, apart from knowing whether I could go on the 1st or 2nd July. I also find out that a boat called Nimrod, based in Kinlochbervie acts as a safety vessel for the Navy, and the skipper knows all about tides and depths - where to go and where not to go. Now it was too late to sail further north anyway, and if I got to say Sandwood Bay, I may be stuck there for 2 days, so better to stay on the campsite.

Thursday July 1st

The biggie. The shipping forecast is perfect, with a south westerly wind, force 3 to 4. My phone call to the Coastguard was promising - The Navy have finished and I am clear to go round Cape Wrath. So I was ready to go by 7.00, and by 9.00 I had passed Handa Island, Loch Laxford and was well on my way to Kinlochbervie where I intended to land.

The puffins are out in force today, disappearing underwater as I get near them. So first it's puffin then it's nuffin. Apparently the collective name for them when they are breeding is a "Stuffin of Puffin".

I heard a dolphin blowing behind me and looked round to see not a dolphin, but something much larger. It turned out to be a Minke Whale, and must have been at least 20 feet long. It kept surfacing for about 15 minutes always about 10 feet from me. Unbelievable! I was sad but glad when it left. Everyone tells me they are harmless, but has anyone told them that?

I landed at Kinlochbervie, but was in the northern harbour where I found myself all alone. I beached and walked up the bank, and could see the main harbour actually in Loch Inchard. It was easier to jog over there rather than sail Oops around the headland, beating all the way past the cliff, then into the harbour.

I found Nimrod, but there was nobody aboard, so I asked someone on a large yacht if they had any charts I could pore over for a few minutes. Klaus and his friends welcomed me aboard, and after finding out what I was up to, Klaus had to have a sit down and a stiff whisky, as did all the others. I declined, but I did have a lemonade, to steady my nerves after the whale encounter. I would dearly have loved to have had the whisky though. They came round Cape Wrath the night before, and couldn't believe I was even thinking about doing it on a Laser. Their computer had all the info I needed. It confirmed for the umpteenth time that I needed to go round at 4.30, which was two and a half hours before high tide at Ullapool. Their charts also confirmed that as the shallow bits wouldn't affect me I could get really close to the headland, and as I came round, would be in the shelter of Clo Mor, and the tide would take me eastward towards Durness. A good plan, that seemed to be watertight, and as I left, they had another whisky to wish me "Bon Voyage". (I'm not sure how they say that in German). I legged it back to Oops, and off I went.

As I sailed out past Oldshoremore, I spotted about seven yachts going the same way as me, which was comforting. They were heading further out to sea, but I hugged the coast all the way past Sandwood Bay and right up to the Lighthouse at Cape Wrath. As I rounded the Headland, in surprisingly innocuous seas, I could see all the yachts turning eastwards, but now they were behind me. I could hear them talking on the radio about me - "Where did he come from" etc. and I was making good headway, past a small sandy bay that I had planned on landing at, as it is the most remotest bay on the mainland. I decided to crack on however, and was fairly close to Clo Mor, which is just awesome. It is 900feet of vertical cliffs straight into the sea, and the highest on mainland Britain. As I was marvelling at this sight, I began to feel the wind rising - it wasn't supposed to do this, but Oh dear a sudden squall laid me flat, and immediately Oops turned turtle.

There were two things that worried me about this trip:
1. A squall hitting me whilst too far from a beach to land and reef, and
2. Something going badly wrong with the boat whilst in a dodgy position and therefore needing to be rescued.

The wind eased, so I righted her quickly, but another squall hit and I was over again. By now one of the yachts was on its way to me, taking the sails down as he came. Later, Pat, the Skipper of my rescue boat *Morag Mhor* said that he was hit by the same squalls, and they registered 30knots, but fortunately his boat was ever so slightly bigger than mine, and could handle it better. I got Oops up again and said I was OK, but something wasn't quite right. The gooseneck had ripped out of the mast, and I watched as it fell towards Davy Jones's locker. I hailed the yacht and said I would be grateful for a tow. By this time we were drifting at about 5 knots towards Garvie Island, which is the Island that the Navy has tried to demolish over the last few years.

A line was thrown to me and I had to do something sharpish. Oops was again on her side, and Pat was telling me to tie the rope to any ******g thing so he could get away from the looming Garvie Island. The line wasn't very strong and it wasn't ideal being tied to the toe straps. I clambered aboard their yacht and away we went for about 200yards until the line snapped. I lowered myself onto Oops as they got near to it, and I was in the drink again, and the rudder was the only thing I could get to tie anything on - let's hope this works. I said "try to keep going really slowly without any sudden acceleration". As she had turned turtle again, the sail, mast, bags, etc, right under the water were making the strain too much. I got back onto the *Morrag Mhor*, and again we carried on like this, for about a quarter of a mile, then "twang" the rudder, and tiller joined the gooseneck at Davy Jones's locker. We were out of danger now so I was able to secure a rope properly this time, but I could see the pound notes mounting up before my eyes. By this time the world and his wife knew that Ron was in trouble, judging by the merry banter between the flotilla of yachts on the VHF radio. The Coastguard interrupted, to ask if it was a Mr Pattenden being towed, and said he was sending a Landrover with flashing lights to Durness to indicate the best place for a landing. Jill, Pat's wife said "How about a nice cup of tea, and some choccy biscuits". I often say to myself whilst sailing Oops –"I think I'll put her on Autopilot and go below and put the kettle on!" As we got into Sango Bay, we could see the lights on top of the Landrover, so we anchored up, and got the tender into the water. It was only a two minute job to attach a line to Oops, and off we went. I said goodbye to Ewan, Jill and Pat, and thanked them for all their help.

As I landed most of Durness had turned up to help, including a cameraman who I thought may be from the local press, but turned out to be Les, who I had met at Scourie, and just happened to be staying on the camp site here. Everyone was keen to carry the boat up through the sand dunes to the road. "Hang on" I said, "just above high tide will do. I intend to carry on sailing from here once I have got all the bits I need." I was glad to see Les, and when all the Coastguards and locals had gone, he helped me up with my bags to the campsite only a few hundred yards away. We dumped my gear next to his tent, and after a shower, had a wee dram or ten - thanks Les.

At times like this you need to have a "The bottle's still half full" attitude or else you could easily be led into a "**** it let's go home" feeling. Stiff upper lip and all that. Alan Minter once said "Sure there have been injuries and deaths in Boxing - but none of them serious" - how serious can it get?

Friday July 2nd

I was on the blower to the very nice Laser people by nine o'clock, and was told by Matt that their 24 hour delivery service was not a problem. So it was back to the campsite safe in the knowledge that I should be away by Saturday afternoon.

James Keith, the campsite owner was brilliant. He had got wind of yesterday's "incident", and offered any tools I needed to fix Oops - he even donated the campsite fees to The Prostate Cancer Charity. The campsite is great, with a brand new shower block with nice tiles and inset lighting, more like you'd expect in The Hilton rather than a campsite. There you are, James I told you I'd give your site a plug. Seriously though, if you have to be stuck anywhere Durness is as good a place as anywhere, if only it would stop raining!!

Sadly I got the inevitable phone call in the afternoon from Matt to say "Sorry, but they don't go that far on a 24 hour delivery, it will be with you on Monday though".

CHAPTER 11

DURNESS TO LYBSTER

<u>Saturday July 3rd</u>
I got a few maps from the Tourist Information Office, and prepared for a walking weekend, after doing a few jobs on Oops.
First though I decided to go back to Cape Wrath, with Les and his wife, but this time by ferry across Loch Eriboll, then by minibus (how tame). Clo Mor looks just as awesome from the land as from the sea. The mini bus driver told us that all the Nato bombing is done on Garvie Island, near my "incident", but a few years ago the Americans decided to bomb an island near Sandwood Bay, about 20 miles in the wrong direction. I guess the house prices are cheap around here, but I'm not so sure about the insurance though.

<u>Sunday July 4th</u>
I did a bit of walking and discovered that Balnakeil was the site of a rocket-warning station until 1955. At the tip of Faraid Head there is the naval station, where observers can see how accurate the bombing is going. I couldn't get into the base, but it must be a spectacular sight to see all the bombs whistling in towards the target. I walked to Smoo Cave, but just missed the guided tour, and only looked around the outer cave which was still quite impressive. Then it was back along a footpath across the moors to the campsite.

<u>Monday July 5th</u>
Today's the day! I phoned at 10.00, only to be told that the bits won't arrive until Tuesday. Remember what I said about half full bottles - mine was looking decidedly half empty!!! Still at least I know, so I didn't waste the day waiting.
More walking, during the day, and I had a great evening in the pub with some of the Coastguards who helped with the boat on Thursday.

<u>Tuesday July 6th</u>
I phoned again at 10.00, only to be told "It should be with you today". I asked "Can you phone the van driver for anything more concrete than that". The reply was "Sorry Sir, we can only do that once it is considered to be late". I remarked "I consider a 24 hour service to be late after 100 hours, don't you" (don't lose your temper Ron). "Oh perhaps you're right sir, I'll get onto it, and ring you back". Was the reply.

I never did find out if she did get on to it, but the bits did arrive at about 1.00. James was as excited as I was, and with the help of his drill, everything was completed and I set sail at 3.00.
The wind wasn't very strong, and I had a job launching into the big swell. Anything northerly produces big waves here, as there's nothing to flatten them out right up to the North Pole. I managed to get to Strathy, but the wind died and I had to paddle in - arrived at 10.30 - then I had to leg it 2 miles to get a signal on the phone to let Coastguard and Hilary know I had landed. Back to put up tent - midnight - something to eat at 1.00am.
Did you know that Princes Hot Dogs are made from "mechanically recovered chicken", asleep by 1.01. There are now two new tests to see if you are brain dead - 1. You start reading the Readers Digest, and 2. You start thinking of going more than ten miles on a Laser.

Wednesday July 7th
I was up early to try and get to Thurso, as I have decided to come home for a few days R. and R., and that is about the only town with a train service. I legged it 2 miles to phone the Coastguard and tried to leave at 8.00, but big surfing waves were rolling in, with very little wind. I need to walk out further than the breaking waves before hopping aboard.
The trouble is that it is in about 10 feet of water. I tried middle of beach, east end, west end, and gave up for an hour. I tried all three again. I then tried launching on the far east in a small river, under cliffs - a bit dodgy but I nearly made it. One last attempt and I was off at 11.30. Still little wind but I made reasonable progress.
I reached Dounereay which is a blot on the landscape - the first nuclear power station in Britain. At the time they discovered that 1 ton of Plutonium produces 18,000,000,000 units of electricity as apposed to 2,400 units using 1 ton of coal.
Just after this I was greeted by about 5 or 6 dolphins, which were about the most lively I have seen (must be radioactive) - it was like a circus, jumping just for pleasure. One came at me from port side and I thought was going to hit but it veered away and leaped over the bows about three feet in front and three feet high. If only I had a hoop and a top hat.
I managed to reach Thurso but was advised to leave Oops at Scrabster which is a large harbour 3 miles around the bay. When I arrived I discovered that it is also the home of Pentland Firth S.C. I managed to get into the locked boat park, by phoning a club official and obtaining the combination lock number, once I had explained what I was doing. It was then much more secure, as there must be hundreds of people who want to pinch a Laser that looks like it is on its last legs. I went back to Thurso to get my train ticket, and work

out what time to get the train. If I don't get the 6.15, I won't make it home tomorrow night.

Thursday July 8th to Tuesday July 20th

Up with the lark, and on my way. I will be back here on the 20th July after a good rest. (There was much muttering about decorating at home to be done, so maybe I'll resume my adventure earlier).

Before I leave though, this bit is directed at the Laser people, and any of you non-boaty types will probably not know what the hell I am talking about, for which I apologise.

Before I started, I asked various people for advice including ClubLaser Direct Parts. All parts were in stock and a 24 hour delivery service was available anywhere on the mainland. (Don't break anything on Mull or in fact anywhere in Scotland, because that appears to be not on the mainland????) I was also given two bits of advice from their sailing advice line, both of which I have ignored. They were:

1. Don't do it!!!

That was like a red rag to a bull, and not the first time I have heard that one.

2. Take a radial rig. (This has a smaller mast and sail).

I don't understand that one. In my experience 70% of the time the wind is light or force three to four, in which case a smaller sail would be inappropriate.

10% of the time it may get a bit hairy but you should be able to spill enough wind until you can reef in.

10% of the time looks dodgy so reef down to radial size or less.

10% of the time, either do not think of going out as wind too strong, or reef down to pocket handkerchief size.

That makes 100% - where is the advantage of a radial rig. You could say the cut of the sail makes it more user friendly, but that only occurs on 20/30% of the time when you reef.

Thinking now about racing - the same arguments apply. If you are in a ten race series, and under (what is it) 11 stone, seven races you will have the advantage (light winds), three races - reef if you are allowed (not sure about rules here). If not you will have to use full sail - reach twice rather than run, come about rather than gybe. OK you may not do well in these three races but you should have done enough in the other seven to win the series. If rules do allow, reef in two races down to about radial size. The last race where it is blowing a hooley, reef to pocket handkerchief size, and you will win the race, as you will be the only finisher. You will be racing with the big boys and not in a smaller handicap class where you may be the only radial sailor.

Come on ClubLaser - defend your advice on using a radial rig, or is it just a way of making people buy an extra mast and sail? Whilst on the subject of cost, why don't you make an upper mast repair kit rather than make us buy a new one?

I have broken a few – usually from heavy beaching. They always break at the same place on the top mast, and can be easily repaired with a small length of an old mast, an internal sleeve, five or six pop rivets and it's as good as new. You will probably say it is now out of class as it has been tampered with. OK so supply a repair kit that is acceptable. It should cost £20 - 30 as apposed to £96 plus postage, and you can carry it around on trips like I am making, as it is so small. Even if you don't own a pop rivet gun, they are only £15, and a very useful tool to have around. You can make a number 1,2,3,4 and probably 5 repair kit before a new mast is required.

I started this trip with a number 1 repaired mast. I broke one at Sennen Cove (big surfing waves) which I repaired in about 20 Minutes (with the help of RNLI's electric drill.) I still have two more repair kits. So I can repair four times as apposed to £400 + for new masts each time, and the inconvenience of waiting two days for delivery. Goose necks now. These usually get ripped out pulling all six rivets and dropping to the bottom of the sea (admittedly only in hairy conditions.) Can it not be redesigned so that it wraps around the mast and then reposition the rivets. I am always available to act as a consultant to think about the poor design of the hole in the hull for the mast!!!

Can you think about using a different courier so that a true 24 hour service is available, and not the 100 hour service I got. In this day and age weekends should not be relevant. OK it will cost more but if you want it quickly then you pay the price.

Sorry if it sounds like I am having a go, on what is a fabulous bit of kit, but things can be improved in small ways - you need a fresh look at times by people who sail them.

That is the end of Lecture. As Arnie would say "I'll be back".

And sure enough I was back. It was good to be home for a few days - I really needed to step back, and think about all things non-laser. It was beginning to do my head in. A bonus was that I did not have to do any decorating – Hilary was only joking. So I arrived back in Thurso late on the 20th.

I managed to catch a Haggis and had some chips with it, whilst walking back to Scrabster, where I let myself in to the boat park. Thanks for the use - it's a pity I didn't meet any of you.

Wednesday July 21st

I was up early and keen to go. A Grampian TV cameraman and interviewer arrived at 8.30 and took shots of me preparing and rolling Oops down to sea. They then interviewed me and took some footage of me going back and forth in the relative calm of the sheltered bay. I left and went across to Dunnet Head which is another headland that I was not looking forward to. You have to go on the flood tide or you will never make it. This is the furthest northerly point on the mainland - two miles nearer the Arctic than John O'Groats. There were some pretty monstrous waves but I got through OK.

I got to Mey Castle, the Queen Mothers favourite home. I can understand why - a lovely old turreted building, especially when seen from below and offshore. It was originally called Barrogill Castle, and dates from the 16th or early 17th century.

The next challenge was to get through The Merry Men Of Mey, a notorious tide race that can reach an incredible 25 knots. It is the wildest of the Pentland Firth's tide-races, and seems to boil the sea between St. John's Point, and the distant island of Hoy. The Admiralty guide, *North Sea Pilot* warns that "The extreme violence of the race, especially with west or north west gales can hardly be exaggerated". So you can see it isn't exactly a walk in the park. When I hit it, I had no control over the rudder and went about a mile unable to fill the sail, as I was being swept along faster than the wind. Eventually I gained control as it eased. I headed into Gills Bay and hugged the coast (and myself in relief) till I reached Kirkstyle, where John De Groot is buried in the 13th century Canisbay Kirk. He was a Dutchman who died in 1568, and gave his name to the village of John O'Groats. It was getting towards the end of the tide so I daren't go further. I landed at the camp site, in John O'Groats and signed the Lands End to John O'Groats log book in the pub, much to the bemusement of four cyclists just starting their challenge - they will be at Lands End probably in a week or so.

I spoke to an ex-coastguard from Eastbourne who now runs sightseeing trips round Stroma in a big Rib. He confirmed that once round Duncansby Head on the flood tide it should be OK as the current then sweeps north. He told me to keep well in, but be careful of the shipwreck at the end of Sannick Bay. From John O'Groats you can actually see the famous tide race that I have to go through - the Bore - but not as bad as the Merry Men Of Mey, apparently. It is strange that Land's End is nowhere near furthest south or west, and John O'Groats is nowhere near furthest north or west. I think the challenge should be replaced with Lizard (South), Point of Ardnamurchan (West), Dunnet Head (North) and Lowestoft Ness (East).

There was a fantastic sunset, seen through the pub window.

In theory once I am round this next headland, it should be all plain sailing back home, but little did I know what the fickle finger of fate had in store for me.

Thursday July 22nd
I was up early to get the flood tide at 8.00. I had to drag Oops over some big rocks which took ages and lots more scratches - while a few people stood and watched - no one helped though.
Duncansby Head was actually a pussy cat, but the sea has carved the cliffs into a spectacular series of arches, stacks, and chasms, and the highest of all is Muckle Stack at 297ft is only a stone's throw from the shore. The next tide race called The Rispie goes at a rate of knots past The Knee, which is a lower stack, again only just off the coast. Then I reached Thirle Door, which is a natural archway. Once past here I thought I was home and dry (well only dampish), but Noss Head (ten miles further south) was worse, with huge waves, but little wind. I went past Wick, but the wind died completely and I had decided to paddle back to Wick - only 15 miles done in 11 hours.
It was not all bad news though - I found a Wetherspoons - the first decent pint since Solway Mist, and it was curry night. I met a guy called Ben who worked in The Wick Pickle Factory. He always fantasised about "dipping his Wick" in the pickle slicer and finally did it today. The only trouble was he got the sack. I asked "What happened to the pickle slicer". He replied "She got the sack too". - Nice one Ben.

Friday July 23rd
I was up at 6.00, but the loos were not open, so I had to make other arrangements - do what the bears do. Why are they always locked when I land and still locked when I leave. I discovered the squeezy bottle of condensed milk had leaked - imagine the mess.
The forecast was 3 to 4 south west. That means tacking all the way. It looks stronger than a 3 to 4 but let's try anyway. I got to Ulbster when it increased to about 6. I nursed Oops into Lybster, and made a heavy landing. As they say up here "Ahm no gooin oot in thart agin". It was my own fault really - I should have trusted my gut feeling and stayed put. We don't need enemies when we have ourselves. Lybster is a "model" village with a broad main street founded in the early 19th Century by Sir John Sinclair.
The cafe owner said it was OK for me to camp on his forecourt in the harbour before he left for the night. He came back an hour later excited as he had just seen me on TV. He said he had never met anyone famous before!!!

CHAPTER 12

LYBSTER TO ABERDEEN

Saturday July 24th
It was an identical forecast as yesterday but totally different in reality. There was little wind but a big swell. I made it to Dunbeath at 12.30 and came ashore for a twenty minute run to warm up. I pressed on to Merriedale in the pouring rain. Sudden squalls nearly capsized me, so I decided to call it a day. I only managed ten miles again today.
The north side of Berriedale can only be reached by a rickety wooden footbridge and is a ghost town with about ten deserted and decayed houses, so I was able to change in the dry. I am now eight days behind (I have lost two in the last four). The nearest pub is back in Dunbeath - five miles away. I walked back and had a great afternoon, as all the locals recognised me from TV and I raised some more money for the Prostate Cancer Charity. I had a tough old steak - it must have been a Shergar Burger. I walked back at about 9.00 and thought about sleeping in one of the houses but it looked scary in the dark (wimp) and as it had stopped raining I camped.

Sunday July 25th
It was a good forecast - westerly force 3 to 4. I started off in light winds, and stood off the coast down to Helmsdale.
I could just about see the other side of The Moray Firth, so I decided to go for it. The wind picked up, and I was reaching then running all the way, surfing on top of the, by now, large waves. I thought I'd died and gone to Laser Heaven - superb. The wind was increasing and my back and knees were becoming painful after seven hours of intense sailing, so I pulled into the nearest harbour. Don't push it, quit while you are ahead, and never test the depth of water with both feet. I made up three days today, and am now only five behind.
The harbour turned out to be Findochty and was founded by Thomas Ord in 1716. A cairn commemorates the death of King Indolphus in AD961. He was killed by Norse invaders commanded by Eric the Bloody Axe.
I found out that Lance Armstrong has just won his 6th Tour De France, which shows that cancer can be beaten - fantastic. Apparently the French hate him, but that is probably because he's not French. Two miles from here is Buckie famous for "
"the scampi run" Apparently if you lose a game of pool and haven't got a single ball down, you have to run naked to the Scampi factory and back.

Monday July 26th
I was up early as there is a 3 to 4 westerly backing north. It was behind me all the way. I stopped at Fraserburgh for a warm up run.
I saw lots of gannets picking up long strands of seaweed - why? Surely it is too late for nesting. I have never seen them doing that before - answers on a postcard please. There are lots of seals near Peterhead. They seem to sleep with their noses just sticking out of the water. I didn't spot one laying in the water today and I actually bumped into it. I'm not sure who was more scared him or me - they are no lightweights. I landed at Peterhead in the bay left of the big shipping harbour and right of the yacht marina. Within minutes the harbour master appeared in a Landrover to see if I needed anything. He knew who I was as he'd seen me on TV.
In the last few days my knees have developed sores - I think it is the new sailing over suit which has tighter legs, so I have to put Germolene then Vaseline on before I put on the wet suit. They seem worse today, I don't think it's Kneemonia, and it can't be Amkneesia (I would have remembered that.) I was hoping to reach Aberdeen today for the Hash House Harriers run - but such is life.

Tuesday July 27th
I managed to get hold of my old mate Dave from the Aberdeen Hash who I have known since 1984. I will meet him tonight, hopefully in Aberdeen, but unlikely in this light wind. It was slow going, but I saw lots of dolphins, a really small baby swimming just under mum's tummy – I've never seen one so small. As I'm making no noise in the light wind I am able to creep up to within three feet of the Puffins without them feeling threatened - they are so cute. I have seen most marine life since being on this trip apart from turtles - I saw one in an aquarium once - it reminded me of my schoolmaster - he tortoise.
I paddled at last to Port Errol, past the remains of Old Slains Castle, an impressive 16th century structure that inspired Bram Stoker to do the Dracula thing. Dr. Johnson remarked that "the prospect here was the noblest he had seen" - must have been on the sauce. Reality is an illusion created by alcohol deficiency.
I had a good evening with Dave and Mary. I met them in a pub, and Mary wanted to see my boat, so we drove to the small harbour, and we stood next to Oops. I asked her to point out which boat she thought was mine. She went through about ten before I told her - she couldn't believe it was so small, (or the boat). We arranged to meet again when I get to Aberdeen. I saw a great house name on the way back from the pub - The Langhoose - is that a spoonerism?

Wednesday July 28th

I woke as usual for shipping forecast at 5.30. I heard a noise, and looked out on harbour to see two fishermen creeping along the harbour wall with rifles - it looked like a scene from the Alamo. Then suddenly, Boom - what a great laxative. They came back and told me they had seen me on TV. I asked what they were shooting. They said it was seals in their salmon nets. What can I say, I am not a fisherman and I know seals do a lot of damage but................
I set off in light winds but I managed to do about twenty miles in nine hours. I had to stop half way for a warm up run - is it really July or have I gone into a time warp to November? I pulled Oops up onto the beach in Aberdeen near to some public loos.
The attendant boiled a kettle for me to have a wash and said he would keep an eye on Oops as I am going to Dave's for a meal and shower. You guessed it; he had seen me on the telly. Fame at last - As Tony Hancock said in the blood doner sketch when told he had a rare blood group - "I always knew I was somehow different from the rest of the herd".
My tent's fire precautions blurb says "Do not use naked flame except in designated cooking area". It's six feet by four feet. Should any of you pop in for a cuppa please ensure you make it four inches from the left hand side of the door. Be careful not to bump into the bathroom which is a two inch square area just behind.

Thursday July 29th

The forecast is south east 3 to 4 later 5. It's always a bit dodgy here with a south easterly wind as there is a big swell. I went to doctors once - I had trapped my todger in a door - I said could you stop the pain but keep the swelling..... Anyway I decided to go shopping and have a decent breakfast as I was in a big town, and the loo attendant would look after Oops for me.
I got back at 11.00 to find that various camera toting people and the police had been around. The wind was not too strong but there were enormous waves. I reefed anyway and set off. It was the right decision but three miles later there was no wind and I was going backwards, so I decided to go back to Nigg Bay just south of Aberdeen.
I came in at a snail's pace but there were some big waves still around. This looks like Sennan Cove I thought and sure enough over I went - another broken mast, and another split sail - unbelievable. This time I smashed into some rocks as well but no real damage.
I pulled Oops up above the high tide, and called the Coastguard to let them know I'm OK. I explained what happened and they sent out Mike and a colleague armed with a drill - on repair duty. We had a laugh fixing mast and I said I would add them to my mailing list. They took some pictures of me

and the boat for their website. Do you struggle to get it right initially? If at first you don't succeed - avoid sky diving.

Friday July 30th
There's no chance of sailing today. When the weathermen say variable less than force 2, just turn over and go back to sleep. I tried to do some emails, but failed as usual. There is something seriously wrong with my address book. I can do the writing stuff, but I have to leave the distribution to Guy. He's good with that sort of thing. Then I got bored, so off to the pub for yet another one or two.
Confucius he say "Our greatest glory is not, in never falling but in rising every time we fall"

CHAPTER 13

ABERDEEN TO ST. MONANS

<u>Saturday July 31st</u>
I was up early, with not too much of a hangover. The forecast was northerly with less than a force 3. I decided to go for it. At least the wind was behind me. It was OK for about five miles then it changed to southerly (still less than force three).
I was tacking and paddling, but nowhere to land until I reached Stonehaven.twelve miles in eight hours. Still at least there is a sailing club with hot showers. Decided to warm up first and had a five mile run to ease out all the joints. Everyone in the club went home by 5.00, and they had no bar (what sort of club is that). Thanks for the shower though. Fortunately there was a pub nearby, so it's not too bad.
A Scotsman in the pub was having a go about the English until he heard my voice - A closed mouth gathers no feet.

<u>Sunday August 1st</u>
Three months gone and just over three quarters done - so I hope to be back before the end of August. Not if we get too many days like today though. I couldn't see the end of harbour and there's no wind. I set about a few jobs on Oops and went for a long walk to Dunnottar Castle, which is a formidable stronghold, built in the 14th and 16th centuries. It defied the English Army for eight months in 1651-2. Cromwell's troops were hoping to capture the Scottish Crown, Sceptre and Sword of State which were hidden in the Castle. But the regalia was smuggled out in a fishwife's basket, and hidden in Kinneff Church, six miles south. The only thing I could find out about Stonehaven is that it was the birthplace of R.W. Thomson, the inventor of the Pneumatic tyre. I think he was known locally as Jo Blob.
The sailing club were racing (at a snail's pace) in the afternoon so I was able to nip in for another shower.
I'll bore you a bit more now, talking about waves. Waves around Headlands are pretty frightening on such a small craft, but only really dangerous when they are steep and, compared to the boat length, close together. This happens when waves run against the wind or headlong into swift tidal currents. When waves become steep their tops are blown off and the water spills forward creating foam which we see as "White Horses".
The highest wave reliably observed was in the Pacific in 1933 at 112 feet high. Every year waves of 50 feet high appear off Land's End. Scientists

calculate that once in 50 years waves of 90 feet high may be generated off Land's End and off Peterhead. Fortunately both are now behind me.

Now I'll bore you about chocolate. Mars have figured prominently for the last 40 years in all the stupid things I have done. They are a great source of instant energy. It has to be Mars though; Snickers lost all credibility when they changed from the much more macho name "Marathon". Snickers sounds too much like underwear, although I suppose we all want to eat what's in them. Peanuts should, in my opinion, only be eaten salted with copious amounts of beer. I have always had Mars bars with me when walking, skiing, hang gliding, mountain biking, squash, motor cycle trials, sailing and running. I equate a Mars to 10 miles running, therefore The High Peaks Race = a 4 Mars Race, The South Downs Way Race = an 8 Mars Race, The West Highland Way Race = a 10 Mars Race, and The Grand Union Canal Towpath Race = a 15 Mars Race. I dread to think how many I have consumed since 1st May this year. It's a good job they are only 35p each.

Did you know that a mini Mars makes an ideal ordinary Mars for midgets and a normal Mars makes an ideal Maxi Mars for them?

A Maxi Mars makes an ideal normal Mars for Giants, whilst a normal Mars makes an ideal mini Mars for them. So you see Mars caters for everyone.

Sorry I'm rambling again, it must be my age. The next challenge I'll do for Outsimers, if only I could remember how to spell it. I must be having one of those CRAFT moments (Can't Remember A F...... Thing)

Monday August 2nd

The forecast is not so good - a force 3 south east. In reality much less than that but at least the tide was with me on the flood from 11.00 onwards. Up till 11.00 I hugged the coast to take advantage of the opposite flow in the bays.

I was also able to gaze in awe at the magnificent Dunnottar Castle that I visited yesterday. I made slow progress but managed twenty miles in nine hours, having stopped for a warm up run half way. Some days we are the flies and some days we are the windscreen.

It was cold and misty in the sand dunes near Montrose, but walking along the beach I spotted a Coastguards building. The very nice man let me have a shower there, and we chatted about the meaning of life for a while. I had a couple of beers in town and back to cook in my tent before bed.

Tuesday August 3rd

I woke up cold at 2.00 having fallen asleep without eating. I got into my sleeping bag only to be woken at 4.00 by gentle lapping of waves on the tent. I thought I was chancing it, being only just above last high water, but to go

further up meant I would be on the steep side of a dune. I dragged both boat and tent up a few feet, but I was most uncomfortable, so I got up early and started at 6.00.
The forecast was 3 or 4 but there was virtually no wind at all. Yet again a big swell and it took two hours to get past the breaking waves to launch. I paddled the first two miles till the tide turned and then I managed to get to Arbroath - ten hours to do twelve miles.
No sun, no wind, freezing cold and soaking wet. But every cloud.... there is a Wetherspoons. Wild Cat - 5.1% made in the Tomintoul Brewery - a nice hoppy beer. They do breed them big up here, a huge woman and her husband just came in the double doors in single pile (sorry - file). She must have been four feet tall - lying down.
I bought a waterproof camera so I may get some good pictures? It never occurred to me to buy one of these, I just thought I would never be able to keep a camera dry so there was no point in bringing one, until Ian my son told me about these throw away ones.
I have with me a brilliant book, that's years old and is a guide to every beach, cliff, and headland along the entire length of the British coastline. It is designed to enrich the pleasures of those for whom the call of the sea and the song of the waves are irresistible. Or as Spike Milligan said,
I must go down to the sea again
To the lonely sea and the sky
I left my vest and socks there
I wonder if they're dry.

Wednesday August 4th

Rain, rain, and more rain. I was up most of night bailing the tent out. It stopped raining about 8.00 but now it's a real peasouper with no wind, so no sailing today. I discovered that someone had pinched my fender that I use to get Oops ashore with. I went to buy another and the guy also made me up a sleeve as a stop gap in case I break my mast again. Arbroath is the home of "smokies" salted haddock smoked over oak-chip fires. You can smell it from about a mile offshore. Originally it was called Aberbrothock (at the mouth of the Brothock). The Abbey was founded in 1178 and in 1320, Scotland's Nobles swore Independence from England in the famous "Declaration of Arbroath" in this Abbey. Fishermen up here say it is unlucky to whistle whilst afloat, and if you do you must touch metal (like we touch wood). I whistle all the time - if you are going to do something wrong at least enjoy it. A hundred years ago the fishwives always launched the boats so the men set out "dry–shod". Wimps - I prefer to start moist. Unlike the Aussies - their version of foreplay is "Brace yourself Sheila".

I went to bed early as I wanted to make an early start if the weather is OK. I was woken up about 11.00 by someone kicking me through the tent. By the time I got out they had legged it, but I looked down to see that they had dragged Oops down the beach right over the sail and mast - Animals - not a good place Arbroath. Now the sail is looking even sorrier for itself than it has in the past. I suppose a few more stitches will be required.

Thursday August 5th
I was up fairly early - glad to leave after last night's episode. Force 3 to 4 easterly sounds OK but still foggy. Fortunately I don't have to tack so I can keep the coast in sight about 100 yards off. But first I had to put a few stitches in the sail.
I launched and went past Carnoustie, and Budden Ness. Next bit was a bit tricky as I had to go across the Firth of Tay. It's only about a mile, but I had to watch the compass and pray. Out of the gloom came the big sandbanks that I was expecting.
What I wasn't expecting was the din of hundreds of seals on the bank. As they sense me they all make towards the sea presumably because they feel safer in the water. The trouble is that they are heading straight towards me, which is a bit worrying. They all nearly reach me before they realise that I'm the one that started it. This continued all the way down to St. Andrews. Still I can only see about one hundred yards, and seals flopping into the water all the time. I stopped at St. Andrews and went for a ten minute run to warm up, and asked a local just to confirm that this is in fact St. Andrews. I carried on past Fife Ness which I was expecting to have a big swell, but was as calm as a thing that's ever so calm. I Limped into Crail now down to about fifty yards visibility. At 6.30 I had managed eleven hours and thirty seven miles from Arbroath.
A sailor once came into Crail,
In search of the Holy Grail,
He found a new sport,
Strange you'd have thought,
And he called it "sailing by Braille".
I went for another quick run to warm up then unpacked. I wish Vaseline made a screw top lid - if anyone knows their website – 'ave a word. I had a good look at the underside of Oops and added some more filler. It's looking sadder all the time, still no major cracks thank goodness.
A doctor can bury his mistakes, but an Architect can only advise clients to plant vines. Perhaps Oops needs to be put in a museum.

Friday August 6th

Another rude awakening at 2.00 as the rain was getting through the seams of the tent again. It was still pouring down till 8.00 so I thought I would wait and see if there is any improvement to the flat calm, and thick fog. I decided to go about 11.30, and only made four miles in six hours to St. Monance, but at least the fog lifted and the sun shone. I am warm whilst sailing – there's a novelty.

About twenty people watched me struggle up through knee deep mud. I tried the fender but that just sank. So it was a question of heave one yard, extract feet and place one yard further up - then repeat umpteen times. And still they all watched.

The mud reminded me of the East Grinstead 100th run, when I was referee in the final of the Ladies Mud Wrestling. Needless to say I was the one who ended up naked - it was a cold day too!!!! Don't worry it only seems kinky the first time.

Later the sun burned off more of the mist and I could actually see North Berwick. Hopefully will go straight across The Firth of Forth tomorrow if wind picks up, and the mist stays away.

CHAPTER 14

ST. MONANS TO SEAHOUSES

Saturday August 7th
I was up and ready to go by 7.00. The forecast was good 3 to 4 easterly possibly 5 later. The sun looks as if it will burn off the mist, but no guarantees. Let's go for it - I lost site of the land behind me after about a mile. My eyes were glued to the compass making sure I go due south. After one and a half hours I could see a vague outline ahead and to the left (off the port bow is the technical term Jim lad - avast behind - bloody enormous)
The land to the left turned out to be Bass Rock. What a fantastic sight – 300 feet high and looks like it's covered in snow. As I got closer I could see that the white is thousands and thousands of gannets. This rock has the world's largest single rock colony, and Scotland supports half the World's northern gannets. A truly awesome sight, especially when you realise that their wingspan is 6 feet. Lots of them are in the air and I am lucky not to get hit - The proverbial is hitting the water all around me, but I escaped unshatupon. I hope my snaps come out OK - but I can't see them looking as good as the real thing. If you do nothing else next time you are in Scotland, you really must see Bass Rock. It is a pity I missed the Isle of May about ten miles north, this has more than 70,000 pairs of breeding puffins, and is only 35 miles as the crow (or puffin) flies from Edinburgh.
I carried on past North Berwick - the visibility was getting much better. As I am now close to the coast I can relax and take in the scenery, I could see a fantastic castle. I even took a picture. A prize for the first person to name it!!! You've got it - Tantallon Castle. It's on the brink of a 100ft cliff, protected by a deep ditch and massive rampart. It was built in the 14th century and frequently attacked, during the turbulent years of Scotland's history. It was besieged for the last time in 1651 by General Monk's English Army.
I managed to get to St. Abbs Head but suddenly banks of fog came rolling in. There was nowhere to run back for about eight miles, but St Abbs was only three miles away southwards, so I crept along just fifty yards from rocky shore. I nearly bumped into a rib with divers aboard - they were trying to get the last of their men up. I crept by and they caught me up and asked if I wanted a tow (Cheek!). I declined and got to St Abbs in what was now a peasouper. Twenty minutes later the Rib arrived - they missed the harbour, and carried on for a mile or so before realising. (Don't get smug Ron)
The trouble with St. Abbs is that there is no pub (Shock, Horror). So I legged

it 3 miles to the nearest village. A pretty good day - great progress, but I was so shattered that after a take-away haggis and chips I could only manage a couple of beers before getting back to put the tent on the slipway next to Oops. (What a dear friend.)

Sunday August 8th
There was thick fog again, so no chance of sailing today. I did one or two bits on Oops, then walked to the village of Coldingham, and popped into the Anchor for a quick one at 12.30, and staggered out at about 5.00. The locals had got wind of what I was doing, so I collected some money for the Charity. I had a great laugh with the locals who wouldn't let me put my hand in my pocket. Why am I so sozzled, and I didn't even buy any drinks.
Apparently The Tales of Para Handy by Neil Monro is like their bible up here - I have never read any but they sound fantastic. According to my new mate Donny (who's web site is http://www.d&jcharters.com), he will take anyone out on his boat. But he will only take divers as long as they don't have a compass - cos they always go the wrong way. His dad lived till 103 and drank 1 pint of Cleary (whisky that hasn't been in oak barrels so it is clear like vodka) per day. He had to drink out of the left side of his mouth because the right side had a pipe clamped more or less permanently in place, and always alight - Good man. Donny is trying to emulate him, I think, but he uses Marlboro instead of the pipe (wimp). Donny's stories reminded me of Sir Bernard Miles tales about a character who cut a hole for his pipe, in his gas mask during the war.
I wobbled out of the pub and phoned home. I found out my friend Flipper is back in south London from his travels and is training to be of all things a plumber. He was on holiday with his girlfriend in Limerick once.

A plumber called Flipper from Lee,
Was plumbing a girl by the sea,
She said "stop yer plumbing,
There's somebody coming"
Said the plumber still plumbing – "It's me".
The girl in question was from the West Country, and always appeared to be lopsided.
There was a young girl from Devises,
Whose breasts were two different sizes,
One was so small,
Hardly nothing at all,
The other was big and won prizes.

Monday August 9th
A fisherman in the pub last night said he would wake me at 6.00 - that was when he was starting out. I was already about to go, so I declined his kind offer of breakfast. The forecast was 3 to 4 rising to 5 or 6 south easterly. In reality it was about a half to 1, but with a very lumpy sea. I progressed slowly for about eight miles in almost as many hours. I could see Berwick-upon-Tweed harbour and decided to paddle in. Someone must have thought I was in trouble and dialled 999. The RNLI came out to meet me. I had phoned the Forth Coastguard before leaving, but now I am across the border in ENGLAND!!!!! They failed to let Humber Coastguard know. The RNLI wanted to tow me in which I declined but it was fun trying to beat the river flow with no wind.
Great news - Yachts and Yachting Magazine have agreed to sponsor me with a new Sail, which I shall be using shortly - all my pleading and whinging has paid off.
Apparently Camilla has friends around this part of the world, and Charlie turned up with a hat made of fox-fur. Camilla asked "Why are you wearing that stupid hat?" He replied "Pater asked me where I was going, so I told him - near Berwick-upon-Tweed, and he said, wear the fox hat."

Tuesday August 10th to Thursday August 12th
I am stuck here with visibility about 100 yards at best. Even if I could see anything I ain't going any where as there is no wind.
Wind is like sex - it only becomes really, really important when you aren't getting any.
I will now proceed to bore you about Berwick as I have seen every last inch of it, albeit by Braille.
Between 1147 and 1482 in the border troubles, between England and Scotland, the town changed hands thirteen times. In theory Berwick is still at war with Russia as they were part of Scotland when a peace treaty was signed. Berwick has the best surviving medieval walls in Europe, completed in 1560 on orders from Queen Elizabeth 1st. Lowry loved this area and about 18 of his famous works were painted here. There is a Lowry Trail that takes you past all the sites, but looks a bit gloomy in the fog and rain. I thought I recognised my granddad in one of the paintings – he's the one that looks like a matchstick man.
I wish I could go sailing - even I'm getting fed up with all these stupid jokes. Still I must be patient - The only place where Success comes before Work is in a dictionary.
At least there is a Wetherspoons so some decent ale - Banks and Taylors - Dragon Slayer seemed the best, but who knows after five or six. I'm not as

think as you drunk I am.

I got back to the boat on Thursday night at about 10.00 to find that someone had stolen my wet suit. All I have to say to that person, is "I hope your earholes turn to a...holes and s... all over your shoulders." I phoned the police who said they would come as soon as possible. I put up the tent and waited.

Friday August 13th

That's right Friday the 13th. Eventually at about 1.00 I fell asleep and woke about 5.30. I phoned the Police again and they said they could not find me. Which bit of right next to the RNLI building don't they understand? Anyway they came out, found me, took a statement, and gave me some addresses to try for a new one, which was about as much as I could expect. The weather was still foggy so I was on a mission to get a new wet suit. I found one eventually but only a back zip job. Peter very kindly gave me a discount as I am doing this for Charity. The weather picked up so I decided to leave in the afternoon. I managed to get past Holy Island in very heavy seas but at least the wind was with me. The Holy Island's ancient name is Lindisfarne and was, with Canterbury, the cradle of christianity in England. I put into Seahouses where a few people recognised me. A great night in the pub on Speckled Hen (that is a beer), and an offer of breakfast tomorrow.

CHAPTER 15

SEAHOUSES TO FILEY

Saturday August 14th
I didn't have my usual 2 cups of tea at breakfast, so I won't need to pee whilst afloat (these rear zip wet suits eh!!) The wind should be a force 3 to 4, but turned out to be a force 1 to 2 again. I got as far as Craster after three hours. I just had to go, so I pulled into this small harbour, and as it was quite busy. I had to leg it a quarter of a mile to the public loos. I struggled out of wet suit - Phew - all this just for a pee. I now have a cunning plan - back to the only shop in village - no velcro - so back to the boat. I cut off a velcro strap on my sailing boot. I rummaged around till I find the right place (easier now to find it, as it's a bit warmer). I cut through a seam on my wet suit around the crutch and sewed velcro onto the flap. (It is important to get the scratchy bit in the right place - visions of carrots and cheese graters.) What a simple solution. GUL - listen you could do this and make a better job than me when you make these suits. I haven't met a single bloke who hasn't complained about this problem with rear zips. If you are in a wet suit for more than a couple of hours - nature calls. I assume you could do the same in ladies wet suits; you just need bigger flaps (if you'll pardon the expression.) Now I can go back to drinking as much as I should do, thank god.
Anyway back on board and off I went, much relieved. I only got as far as Amble. Again a big swell coming into harbour and I landed twice in some not very friendly places. Eventually I found a Yacht Club, where I was able to use their shower. There were only three people, so it closed at 9.30. The trouble now is that there has been so much rain, mud everywhere unless you come in to these rivers at high tide. If I hadn't got a shower it would have been very messy. I walked to town and got a pizza.

Sunday August 15th
I left at about 8.00 in the usual light winds coming at me from various directions. I actually fell asleep in the warm sun. The coast is so straight that you drift past towns without realising. I thought I was landing at South Shields, but saw the Sunderland Yacht Club as I came into the harbour.
The only lesson we learn is that we don't learn the lessons. There were a few people still in the club and although they closed at 7.00, they insisted on rustling me up a curry and a beer, and I went away with a packed lunch for tomorrow. Apparently the Commodore was in hospital - he swallowed a

daffodil bulb instead of an onion – he'll be out in spring.

Monday August 16th
Again light south west winds so I left at 8.00 only just making headway against the ebbing tide. It was better when the tide turned and I limped into Whitby. I wanted to get to Robin Hoods Bay, but couldn't risk it as there is nowhere else to land, and I don't fancy drifting in the dark. I landed on a beach opposite a big fairground. I didn't remember it being this busy when I was here last. I went into town and there were literally hundreds of people. Apparently it was the last day of their carnival.
When I got back to the boat, it was cordoned off, as the fireworks were going off quite near here. A great display, but most of the people who gathered on the beach decided to stay the night and lit bonfires.

Tuesday August 17th
I didn't get much sleep, so I was up early to find that the fair had gone. It appears that they are only allowed to stay for 3 days. The wind was supposed to be a 3 to 4 but it died around Robin Hoods Bay.
A fisherman came over to me and asked if I wanted a tow in, as he could see I hadn't moved for about an hour. I declined the offer, and he cut his engine, and we sat chatting about Vintage Motor Bikes (he has 4) and our experiences going through the Pentland Firth. As we were drifting at different rates, he started his engine again and came over to me, and we continued the conversation with him holding mine and me holding his (boat that is) It must have looked really funny seeing us just sitting there. The wind eventually picked up and I made it to Scarborough - just. I landed on the north beach, and the lifeguard said I couldn't stay there, because you are not allowed to land or launch on this particular beach. So I broke both rules then by launching.
I limped into the harbour only to find the slipway blocked, so I had to go out onto another slip on the southern beach. Fortunately there was no lifeguard there.
I walked to town, and had a beer and a meal in another Wetherspoons pub. You have to find a vacant table, then go to the bar and order your food, and give them your table number. When you get back to your table, you usually find that someone else is now sitting at that table, who refuses to budge, so you try to tell the bar staff, who then doesn't know how to handle it, and when the food arrives there's utter confusion - what a great system. They wouldn't let me charge my phone either, even after explaining why I need to plug it in. (More than my job's worth Guv.) It's a shame really because I like the places; they just haven't quite got it right. They spend a fortune on doing

these places up, and then "Spoil the ship for a hap'enth of tar" to use a nautical term. I asked them if they wanted me as a Mystery Shopper, because I could have had a field day telling them what needs doing and would cost peanuts to implement. Sadly they declined my offer.

Wednesday August 18th
It rained most of the night but I slept through most of it as I was so shattered after the Whitby Carnival. I bailed out and set off in the rain. I need to get to Flamborough Head by about 2.00 as that is when the tide turns and floods south. Light winds again and I struggled to get past Filey.
Eventually I got past Filey Brigg and made it into the bay where there is an opposite current. I hugged the coast till almost Flamborough, but the wind was strengthening and I didn't want to go round fully rigged. I decided to reach back to the nearest sandy shore, but unfortunately capsized about fifty feet from shore.
Sadly it was only in about ten feet of water and as it turned turtle and, you guessed it, snap went the mast. Experience is something you get just after you need it. I got her upright, and with now an extremely reefed sail decided to sail directly back to Filey, as there is no other town or village where I could borrow a drill to repair the mast. I was easing her along gently, knowing that any harsh moves would rip the sail and could possibly lose the top half of the mast.
Suddenly the RNLI appeared. Fortunately they were on exercise so were not called out, as I did not need rescuing. They wanted to know my details and I got them to phone Humber Coastguards, who have them. They said they would escort me in and a camera was produced so they now have some good photos of what not to do with a Laser. They were using their big boat so couldn't do anything for me as I came in to land, but I asked if they could have someone in the water to stop me just about knee high so as to not let the mast hit the sand and do more damage. Charles and a lady (sorry I can't remember her name) were there to assist me -Thanks guys.
There was some merry banter was going on - Charles said "Here comes a WAFI." I asked him "What is a WAFI". He said "a Wind Assisted F*****g Idiot" – that's nice.
Anyway he offered to give me a hand and lent me some tools. His dad even came out and lent me a workbench, what more could I need?
The mast was all sorted within a couple of hours, but too late to go until tomorrow, so I was stuck on the slipway for the night.

Thursday August 19th
I had a rude awakening at 4.30 by the fishermen dragging their boats down

with a tractor. I know I can't go till 2.00 as I need to go on the flood. I am a bit worried about the forecast which says "May be up to force 6 later". I got up and repaired the sail which was fortunately only ripped round the mast sleeve. I turned Oops over and put more filler in. the weather looks OK - there is a Dart catamaran in the bay in about a force 3. So all targets met, all systems working, all customers satisfied, all pigs fed and ready to fly. I dragged Oops down by 2.00 and reefed her ready to go. A sudden squall hit her and capsized before I had even put the boom on. I walked over to the Dart sailor, who had just returned to shore and we discussed the meaning of life for a while, then we both took our boats back above the high tide line. He said it may be OK for a jolly in the bay, but there's no way that he would ever dream of going round Flamborough Head, even on a calm day. Ho, Hum - another night in Filey then. I mooched about a bit - went to pub, and met a guy who had helped me down with the boat onto the beach earlier, which obviously led to a couple more beers.

Now I shall bore you about charity. As a lot of you know, I have done quite a few marathons and ultra-marathons for different charities. I think that the website is a brilliant way of getting sponsorship. I wear Prostate Cancer Tee Shirts, but don't like to push it. (I hate people with boxes under your nose). I didn't like going round after events collecting money - it seems too pushy. This way you can give (or not) as you wish. I give to certain charities but don't necessarily want to put into "Save the Whale" or "Sponsor a Donkey". It is a shame that we have to have charities, money should be available for all the things we care passionately about, out of the tax we all pay. We pay 80% tax on petrol - where does it go??? Even the money we buy petrol with has already had income tax taken off it, in some cases by as much as 40%. Having said that, thanks to all who have put into the Prostate Cancer Charity, it is much appreciated.

The next challenge I do will be for Alzheimer's, as that is what my Mum has and is currently in a home for the bewildered. I hate to see her as she is now compared to how she used to be. I know that anything I do won't help her now but it may help my, and future generations. Do you know that more money is spent on breast implants and Viagra than on Alzheimer's research? This means that by 2030 there should be a large elderly population with perky boobs and huge erections and absolutely no recollection of what to do with them!

Then I would do something for the RNLI who do a fantastic job, all voluntarily. If I, as a WAFI have caused problems for them, I apologise. I really don't want them to be called out for me, and I do all I can to stay safe, but the sea is a hostile environment, and problems can occur especially on such a small craft.

What is the nutter going to do next, you may well ask. Well I have some cunning plans. If any rich person is out there who wants to sponsor me I would love to:
1. Sail in the Round the Isle of Wight race on a laser. I was part of the crew (cannon fodder) on the Hoya 60 (The old 60 foot Silk Cut Round the World Yacht) a few years ago when Linford Christie was aboard filming "Record Breakers." I believe there is a class for oldest boat and helmsman. I have an even older laser (no. 7670). The Laser manufacturers can't tell me when it was built, because they only have records back to no. 21000. They think it must have been built in 1973, or earlier. So combined age of helmsman and boat would be about 86 years.
2. I still have to "do Ireland" as I missed out this "little" island this time.
3. I was in New Zealand earlier this year and would love to sail round both Islands. This time I would like to have a land based support crew, rather than doing it unsupported. I doubt whether anyone has done NZ on a Laser, so if there is anyone with deep pockets who would like to sponsor me, obviously your logo on the sail will do you no harm. If I have a land support crew I feel that I would only sail when there is good weather and I can enjoy it rather than sailing when it is not appropriate, just to get the miles done.
The only two things I would take that I am missing this time are
1. An EPIRB (Emergency Position Indicating Radio Beacon) which is obviously a panic button in case things get too bad.
2. If someone can come up with a life jacket rather than a buoyancy aid, that is user friendly and I still can right the boat whilst wearing it.
Charles Baker from Filey, who helped me with my broken mast, has already offered to sponsor me on the Isle of Wight Race and has already, supplied me with wait for it - A Tee Shirt!!! Thanks Charles. He's the one who told me I am a WAFI, but he still wants to sponsor me!!
I have also thought of another challenge. I own a 1959 Royal Enfield Bullet. (A 350cc motorbike in trials trim - we actually used to call them Royal Oilfields for obvious reasons) I wouldn't mind trying to go round Britain on that. Making a combined age of bike and rider = 100 years. The big challenge there would be - how far can you go each day before breaking down.
Anyway that is in the future; first of all I have to get further than Filey.

Friday August 20th
I'm still here in Filey. A chap swims here every day of the year, and I chat with him each morning. (I'm even beginning to be treated like a local - I've been here so long) He said that the expression "All shipshape and Bristol Fashion" comes from sailors around the Bristol Channel where the tide and

weather are so bad that if it ain't tied down it's lost overboard. There is a super loo on the front at Filey, that costs 20p. There is a shower, pot pouri, potted plants, but no piped music. They are the best loos I have been in.
I pitch my tent next to Oops just under a terrace, and was woken up about 12.30 by someone urinating on the tent and shouting abuse. I got up and chased away a couple of kids. They returned once I got back in the tent and hurled stones at me. There was no alternative but to call the police. They were sympathetic but what could they do? (I know what I'd do if I got the little B's).

CHAPTER 16

FILEY TO CROMER

Saturday August 21st
I still can't leave. After hearing the shipping forecast, I went to the RNLI station and asked their advice. There is such a big swell, that you can see about fifty feet of spray coming off the Brigg, and through their binoculars, you can see the enormous waves crashing onto Flamborough Head. All this, with absolutely no wind. They advised against going in these conditions - wait another day. I've heard that one before.
My friends Graham and Paul were coming up to give me some support in my hour of need, and they arrived about lunch time. Oh well just the odd pint or two then. We had a great laugh and Gray took some good photos. They had brought a tent with them but didn't like the nasty hard ground, so they booked into what must have been the best Hotel in Filey (Tarts). We had a slap up meal and by the time I got to bed I was so sozzled I could have slept on a washing line.

Sunday August 22nd
The forecast was better than of late, and the sea looked a bit calmer. I was going to make an early morning 2nd attempt at getting round Flamborough Head. I phoned Graham at six o'clock to let him know, and they both came to the beach to see me off. Gray took some good photo's as I kept trying to launch in the big swell. Unfortunately, the wind was not strong enough to push me with the tide. I really needed to leave at 3.00 but it was not light enough until 6.00.
Anyway I nearly got to the headland by 9.30, but the tide turned and was far stronger than the wind, so back I came to Filey. I couldn't land anywhere else as the swell was still too great along the coast. Charles and all the people I had met were surprised to see me back, but all were sure I would get round later.
I left for a third attempt about 3.00 and success. I got round the headland and made Bridlington by about 8.30, just as a passenger ferry was coming in. It was getting dark, but I had to go about rather than gybe as the wind was getting up. I made it in front of him, but I suspect he was wondering why I didn't go straight in.
As I pulled up David (an RNLI chap) greeted me and helped me up with Oops. He knew who I was as a chap called Roger Oliver has been trying to find me. I was able to shower at the Royal Yorkshire Yacht Club, and while

I was there Roger turned up. He is doing the same as me but in a 24 footer. He left Portsmouth on the 7th May and keeps hearing about me but we have never met. He went round Ireland but was stuck for 5 weeks while I was going up through Wales and Scotland.
POTENTIALLY I should have sailed 112 days, according to my original plan and should have been home on the 20th August. REALISTICALLY I have sailed 78 days so far and have had 36 days not sailing. It is 22nd August and I am still at Filey. A kid came home from school and said to his dad that he had to write something about the difference between POTENTIALLY and REALISTICALLY. He didn't know how to go about it so his dad said to ask his mum, sister, and brother if they would sleep with Tom Cruise for a million pounds. His mum and sister said "yes" immediately, and his brother wasn't so sure but eventually said "yes". The boy went back to his dad and said "I get it, POTENTIALLY we are sitting on 3 million pounds, but REALISTICALLY we are just living with 2 prostitutes and a raving poofter".

Monday August 23rd
I got up in the pouring rain, David had arranged for the local paper to do an article on both Roger and myself. He didn't turn up so David took our details to pass on. No chance of moving today, it was blowing a gale, and it didn't stop raining all day.
I was offered a bed in the bunk room of the Yacht Club, and initially declined, but the rain was so bad that my tent was waterlogged, so I accepted the offer. What a relief for my back which is still playing up after being hit by the Tenby Safety boat, especially laying down, for some reason. This is only the second night indoors, the first being John's house in Dartmouth, which now seems like 20 years ago.
So Ben Ainsley won Gold on the Finn in the Olympics. (4 years ago it was gold on the Laser.) I would love to shake his hand and just touch his gold medals, as he is undoubtedly Britain's and indeed the World's finest sailor. He had to put on 15 kilos to be competitive in the bigger Finn. I would need to put on about 30, as I have lost so much weight. If he was drugs tested they would probably say he had overdosed on Steak and Milk.
And what a terrific performance by our girls in the Yngling. The boat was designed in 1967 by Jan Linge, a Norwegian. A strange name - do you Yngle it or sail it. Perhaps it was used to fish for Ling (similar to cod).

Tuesday August 24th
It seems strange listening to the shipping forecast without the sound of the sea crashing about me. I thought we had no chance of sailing today, but the

forecast was good - a force 3 to 4 south west to west. I walked across to the harbour - it was very misty but I thought it would clear, so I walked quickly back to the club, packed and set off at 8.00. I said goodbye to Roger - he is going to try to get all the way to Wells-next-the-Sea. It's OK for him, as he can sail at night and has an auto-pilot. I made good progress but was hit by a couple of squalls which nearly caught me out. I feel at times that I am "flying by the seat of my pants" (We had a book at work of all of "Ron's" sayings, and that was one of my favourite ones. I wonder if it the book is still around?) I radioed Roger, who was a couple of miles behind, and told him to be careful (not that an experienced helm like him needs my advice). I was hoping to get past the Humber, but I could see lightning and hear thunder in the distance so I decided to stop at Easington just short of Spurne Head.

I walked to the pub where I once again fell asleep at the end of my meal. The Landlady was going to turn the lights off for a laugh. The wheel's going round, but the hamster's dead. Just as I was about to leave, I was invited in to talk to the local Lodge of the Royal Antediluvian Order of Buffaloes. They were all wearing their regalia, but fortunately I didn't have to do a dodgy handshake. They presented me with a cheque for the Prostate Cancer Charity, and I left not knowing how to feel about such "clubs". Then it was back to Oops in the dark and up with the tent. I was asleep by 10.00.

Wednesday August 25th
The forecast was good with a force 3 to 4 westerly up to force 5 to 6 later. It looked gusty and I never like a forecast with a 6 in it. Anyway I reefed down knowing that I should have enough power in the sail as it would be a broad reach. I got across the Humber with no problems, always keeping an eye on the huge tankers coming and going. I stopped just below Grimsby to take out the reef, disturbing the hundreds of seals on the shore. I got to Skegness without incident, and decided that the clouds all looked benign, so I decided to go across the Wash to Hunstanton or further east without reefing. Big mistake - a couple of squalls hit me again and I decided to pinch up into the wind rather than a broad reach eastwards. I made it to Hunstanton OK, but I was really shattered when I landed with all that concentration.

Someone asked me how you would describe most of the trip. I replied "Half a Crown – Sixpence" but I suppose after decimalisation it should now be "10p - 1p" but that's not got the same RING to it.

Thursday August 26th
I was up early again as the forecast was north west force 4 to 5 backing south west 3 to 4. A couple of runners helped me down the long beach with Oops. As the wind was behind all the way I decided to reef. The sea was slight and

I made good progress in reasonably calm seas. By 12.00 the swell was rising but the wind didn't really pick up, so I was quite OK surfing along.
When I got to Cromer I came inshore to see if there were any safe landing places, and suddenly got caught by a large wave which capsized me. I righted her but capsized twice within the next ten minutes. I was getting tired so I decided to go east of the pier thinking that a small harbour would be there. I knew there was a fishing fleet in Cromer. Unfortunately they launch with tractors from the beach, so that was the only answer. I did my usual trick, surfing through the waves, but as I was fully reefed I couldn't control it as there wasn't enough wind. Over it went breaking the bottom section of mast (which to be fair has seen better days) and bending beyond repair, the upper section. I lost my glasses and took a chunk out of my thumb. A couple of people helped me up above High Tide line. I went up to the Lifeguard, who put a dressing on my thumb.
A sudden bang and the local coastguard were launching. I had a feeling it was me they were launching for and the Lifeguard phoned through to say I have been ashore for 10 minutes. The Coastguards came to see me and asked what on earth I was doing out in such seas. They were bemused by my story and didn't know what to do. I said that I was sorry but I had to sort out the mast. I was getting a bit weary of all this and beginning to wish that the fat lady would burst into song. I called my friend Graham and he sorted out a new mast to be delivered in three hour's time. James Borthwick, from the yacht chandlers, drove from Kings Lynn (I think). Great stuff James - you are a Diamond Geyser.
I met Mike, an old colleague from work, who drove up to see me, and had a great evening although very weary. Thanks for driving up to see me Mike, it was just what I needed after such a day.

Friday August 27th
The forecast was not good, but I hung about for a few hours chatting to the local fishermen who also seemed reluctant to go. The fact that they were actually on the beach meant that there was at least a chance of going out. I decided after a while that the waves were too big again so I managed to get an hour on the Library's computer.
I popped in to the Dolphin and had a pint or two of Sunny Jim, a light summer ale at 3.8%, by Robinsons Brewery. Then I unfortunately found out that they also had Theakston's Old Peculiar on so the rest of the day went a bit shall we say Peculiar, but I do remember telling a bloke I was an Agnostic. He said "That's in Eastern Europe isn't it?"

CHAPTER 17

CROMER TO LONDON

<u>Saturday August 28th</u>
The forecast was not bad at force 3 to 4 decreasing to force 2 to 3 south west. There were still big waves and with the wind dead behind, I decided to reef as it is more comfortable on a dead run in large seas. I tried twice to launch but kept getting pushed along the beach in the breaking waves which were out of my depth, getting closer and closer to a groyne. I decided to walk Oops nearer to the pier to get as much shelter as possible.
I made it on the third attempt and flew to Caister, surfing all the way. I landed and took out the reef as I was now on a broad reach, having turned the corner and now going south. Once the tide turned I was going even quicker, past Great Yarmouth and on to Lowestoft. The tides are much easier to figure out down the East coast, they just ebb north and flood south.
As I came in to the Harbour two young lads helped me up on a slipway with Oops. They had seen the big write up that Yachts & Yachting have printed, and pointed me to the Royal Norfolk and Suffolk Yacht Club showers. Coming in to the Harbour, I realised that I have just passed Lowestoft Ness, so I have now been past the furthest South, West, North, and East points of the mainland. After a wonderful shower, it was off to the bar, to meet the other guests who were here for the Javelin Nationals with about fifteen boats. One race was cancelled today, and they were due to have four tomorrow back to back.
I then heard about Kelly Holmes getting her second Gold, and our boys in the 4 by 100 metres - fantastic. I think Paula Radcliffe should have finished her race, even if she had to walk. I can understand her having to stop in the Marathon, as the heat and exhaustion is awful, but there is no excuse in the 10000 metres race. If any of us "mere mortals" were given the opportunity of competing in the Olympics we would crawl over the line if necessary, She wasn't even tired, let alone exhausted, just because she wasn't going to get a medal doesn't mean she should stop running. In most races there are normally only 5 or 6 real contenders but you don't see the others not trying right up to the finishing line. When I tried to run the 145 mile Grand Union Canal Race unsupported in 1997 I was really upset not to have completed it, and swore to do it the next year. Hilary supported me then and she had to walk (along with Tina), the last 20 miles with me so that I completed it. I got a crap time of 47 hours, and came in almost last, but I just wouldn't give up. I always give 100% and in fact when I was at work I used to give 110% every

week. 25% mon, 25% tues, 25% weds, 25% thurs, and 10% on fri. Obviously you couldn't give as much on a Friday as the pub was always beckoning.

Sunday August 29th
The forecast was force 4 to 5 south west occasionally force 6 - veering west. I decided that it looked stronger than that and there was no point in fighting the tide as well as the wind, so I will wait till the tide turns about 12.30. I watched the Javelins start their races, but they were struggling to beat into the wind with the big waves. One race was cancelled and by the third race several boats had given up. A good time to adjourn to the bar and discuss for the umpteenth time "The Meaning of Life" No sailing today, but I read an interesting article about Bruce Kirby, a Canadian who designed lots of boats including the Laser in 1969. Amazingly it is still up there with the best, with no changes. (not even the few that I recommended to the Laser guys.) Can you imagine a 1969 car design still going strong. I suppose the mini had a good run, but the new mini bears no resemblance to the old one.

Monday August 30th
The forecast was even worse today with a north westerly force 5 to 6 with 7 occasionally. A good direction though, and I decided to reef further than I have in the past and go for it. At least there was no swell, now, as these westerlies flatten out the sea. There were plenty of beaches and I could keep right in and land quickly if I had to.
I left at 6.30 having had to pull Oops round chest high onto moorings. The slipway was too narrow to turn her round to rig into the wind. I came out of the harbour with much trepidation, but she was responding well. It is amazing how even in a force 7 she is so responsive with such little canvas showing. I shot along to Aldeburgh by high tide. I spotted the sailing club and went in for a rest.
I thought about staying until low tide, but the club members told me where the sand banks were and that if you avoided them and hugged the coast, you can usually cheat the tide. I was just about to leave when one of the guys came up and gave me £20 for the charity. He said it had only just sunk in how long I had been sailing, and wished me good luck. He said "Look out for the sweeping radar scanners at Bawdsey, that's where Radar was invented, and the Early Warning system that played such an important role in the Battle of Britain."
The wind eased in the afternoon, but became squally in two huge downpours, with thunder and lightning, so I was glad I left the reefs in. I got to Felixtowe, and as there are now lots of breakwaters and groines around,

landing was not such a problem. Spike Milligans army friends said they were concerned about the landing in Italy during the Second World War, but Spike said "Don't worry I'll hoover it tomorrow".
I met my sister, Barbara, and Jim' in Felixstowe for a drink and a meal and was glad to get to bed after another tiring day.

Tuesday August 31st
I woke up early and remembered that I sent a text to Hilary, but I hadn't phoned the Coastguard to let them know I had landed safely, last night. I quickly phoned them and they noted it. I asked if anyone had contacted Hilary, or was anyone out looking for me. NO. So why am I bothering to phone them??????? This goes back to my Tenby problem - they don't have a duty of care. I can't believe that they have a log of someone at sea who should have checked in before dark. I haven't, but they don't do anything about it. They are the ones that insist I phone them for safety reasons.
The forecast was north west force 4 to 5 becoming variable 3 or less. I had a good sail right up to the Crouch Estuary. I decided that rather than beating up into Burnham, I'd go round Foulness and hope to get past Maplin Sands, and Southend. I should have taken notice of the forecast as the wind eased and I only got as far as Shoeburyness, nearing low tide. Here the tide goes out about a mile. (Shades of Blackpool).It was getting late, so I started to drag Oops as far as I could in the shallows (two to three inches) then brought the bags ashore, when the tide went completely.
Gael, the editor of Yachts &Yachting Magazine, arrived on the beachwith my new sail, but we were getting eaten alive by mossies, and as Gael came straight from work, her clothes were not suitable to help with Oops, but Justin, Darren, and Richard (kite surfers) offered to help. When we got close, Keith (another kite surfer) arrived with a van and trolley so it wasn't so bad. Thanks guys, I would have been there for hours without you. We tied Oops to a fishing boat, which was at anchor, so I could get off tomorrow before high tide. Just time for a beer and fish and chips, then to bed shattered again.

Wednesday September 1st
Again the forecast was not good - variable force 3 or less, then south 3 or 4. I had to wait until nearly high tide, and I managed to get under way at 12.00 (a good plan tying to the fishing boat) A good run with what was left of the tide past Southend, and managed Stanford Marshes by 6.00. I was hoping to get further up the Thames, as I am going to sail up to Tower Bridge, to a reception with the Charity people, and my old colleagues from work. I tied Oops to a concrete pipe so I could get off early. I then had a long walk to Stanford - Le - Hope where I met another colleague Jim for a drink. (Back

into home territory now, where I know a few people.) I read an article about some of the strange names used in some Olympic events. I thought it must be daunting for non sailors when we start talking about burgees, leech, luff, outhaul, downhaul, mainsheet, jib, gybe, running, beating, reaching, kicking strap which now is called a vang unless it is upside down, in which case it's called a gnav. And last but not least the good old cunningham. My solicitor was called Mr. Cunningham. He was one of the partners in the firm called Hunt, Blunt and Cunningham.

Thursday September 2nd
I have got to get this right or I will be floating up and down the Thames all day. The Forecast was force 3 to 4 S backing SW, which was pretty irrelevant really, as the tide is the only thing that really counts going up the Thames. I started at 5.30 which was sadly half an hour too late as I had to push Oops through knee deep mud into the receding tide. I made it to Gravesend (what a great name - very descriptive) against the tide. Once the tide turned I knew I would fly, but would 6 hours be enough to get to Tower Bridge. The answer was yes - just. On the way I got a text from Lisa saying I should come home ASAP as Tina (our Jack Russell) was poorly. I made it to St Katherine's Dock by about 3.30 where I met the Prostate Cancer Charity Ladies (that doesn't sound right - it should be men.) and Guy, Nige, Gray, Tone, and the two Mikes. Thanks for the welcome guys. A few beers later then off home.

Friday September 3rd
Tina has been at the vets for 2 days and we were allowed to stay with her all day. Finally Hilary decided that enough was enough, and it was kinder to let her go. We both cuddled her as the injection worked. She came with us everywhere. She loved coming out on the laser, and even had her own life-jacket when we went cruising in Poole Harbour, and out to Studland. Me and my three girls - Hilary, Tina, and Oops. She came with us Round Britain by Tandem in 2002 in a basket on front. We miss her.

CHAPTER 18

LONDON TO DOVER

Saturday September 4th to Monday September 6th
At Home

Tuesday September 7th
I'm off again - up at sparrows fart and Hilary drove me to the station for the 5.15 train. I listened to the shipping forecast at 5.45. north east force 5 to 6 gusting 7. Not good, but I should be OK as I will be relatively sheltered in the Thames. I will reef down quite a lot as the tide will take me for 6 hours on the ebb. When I got to London St Katherine's lock was about to open up for a Thames Barge to exit so I followed it into the lock. Oops looks pathetically small next to such a large craft. The barge was only going into the Poole of London, so was waiting for Tower Bridge to open, once we were out into The Thames. I decided that having come this far I may as well go through both Tower and London Bridges, just for fun. The current was very strong against me but a broad reach in the good breeze was not a problem. As I came under London Bridge I could see all the London workers streaming across above, just like I used to. I now don't do WORK - that's a four letter word, and you know how I hate swearing.
Anyway back through the bridges and I met the barge coming through the now open Tower Bridge. Quite a sight, but it would be even better if he was under full sail. The journey down the Thames went smoothly, but it takes longer than you think, and just after the QE2 Bridge, the tide turned and I was now underpowered with the reef in. Unfortunately there was nowhere to beach and take out the reef, so I kept as close to the southern bank as possible, out of the main current. I went past the Tilbury to Gravesend passenger ferry and found a small beach right next to an old church, on the edge of town. I pulled Oops above high tide line and went in search of you know what. That's right a Wetherspoons, and as it is Tuesday, it's steak night. A really nice sirloin and a few pints of Abbot Ale, with Paul (my motor cycle trials rider friend) then back to put up the tent in the dark. Great Expectations was written here by Dickens. Gravesend got its name because it was here that all the victims of the London plague were buried in 1565.

Wednesday September 8th
A north east force 4 to 5, veering south east was forecast so I will be sailing right into it again. It felt stronger than 4 to 5, so again I put in a reef, and

headed off eastwards. After about a mile I decided that I need to reef even further so up I went on the mud and another couple of turns round the mast. I can now only see 3/4 of the window in the sail. I made good progress until 1.30 when the tide turned. I was near Canvey Island and tacking back and forth kept bringing me back to the same place, in the strong current. I decided not to attempt any further, because I didn't want to get caught on any of the sandbanks that are everywhere around here. At least it is only a short pull up the beach here on Canvey Island. I had to drain Oops out before pulling up. She has sprung a leak again. The mast hole looks suspect, so out with the good old Plastic Pudding. Poor old Oops was built in 1978, and has had so many fillings this year that she has been banned from the Olympics - she tested positive for Steroident. The river Thames is a horrible brown colour even as far out as here. T.S. Eliot wrote of the Thames "The River sweats oil and tar". The Lobster Smack Inn on Canvey seemed to be beckoning me. (This inn appeared in Great Expectations.)

Thursday September 9th
The forecast was east/ south east force 4 to 5. So I was tacking again all the way. I left at 8.00, just on high tide, so at least the current will help me. I got to Minster, past The Medway estuary, but I was getting tired so I decided to reef again and let the current do most of the work (you don't have a dog and bark yourself do you). I made reasonable time to Herne Bay when the tide turned and the wind eased. I landed to take out the reef, and also checked that the leak was fixed (surprisingly - yes). From here you can see the twin towers of the ruined church at Reculver, which was founded by King Egbert of Kent in 669. They are such an important landmark that in 1809 they were repaired after gale damage even though not in use. The church stood back from the sea until the early 19th century, when the sea wall was sold to the company building Margate Pier. I limped along to Minnis Bay, where I was guaranteed a bed for the night at my old friend Jill's house. (She's not old, we are just old friends. In fact I'm sure she is only about 25!!!) Anyway she lives in Canute Road, and it was around here that the king ordered the sea to retreat. Everyone at the time said "What a stupid Canute" (not sure about the spelling). It was on this day in 1923 that Sliced Bread was invented. It was said at the time to be the best thing..........EVER.

Friday September 10th
Guess what, the forecast is for a south westerly force 3 to 4 then veering south west force 4 to 5. I don't believe it - against me again. I started beating in the very light wind past Margate. Then I sailed past some exotic sounding bays, Palm Bay, and Botany Bay. In reality they were not exotic at all.

Beating round North Foreland, and as I am now travelling SW, (you've guessed it) the wind has veered south west. I was now beating past Broadstairs, Described by Dickens as "one of the freshest, freest watering places in the world." Bleak House, where he wrote some of his best known books, stands prominently to the north of the small bay, and just below is the quaint pier which dates back to the time of Henry VIII. I was still beating past Ramsgate and into Sandwich Bay. The town is best known for John Montague, an 18th century Earl of Sandwich, who was such a devoted gambler that he couldn't bear to leave the table for meals so he ate beef between slices of bread, thus originating the 'sandwich'. The bay played an important part in "Goldfinger" where James Bond and his gold-crazed foe played their epic game. The wind was strengthening so I reefed down again, beat past Deal, where it eased, so out with the reef, (in and out like a fiddlers elbow.) and decided to try for Dover. I got near to the entrance of the harbour, but there was so many ferries coming and going, that I radioed the Harbour Master to ask if it was safe to cross the Harbour entrance, as I was struggling against the tide. He said "Stand by, and I'll send a pilot to escort you across." We got across the Eastern entrance, but then the wind died and it was embarrassing tacking back and forth going nowhere with the pilot boat tracking me. I think he was getting bored with this WAFI, as he eventually offered to tow me in the Western entrance, so I could land on the beach. I gratefully accepted as it was getting dark, and I could be ages getting past the entrance. About 5 minutes later I was on the shore and waved them goodbye. I dragged Oops up past the high water line, phoned the Coastguards, and Hilary. Then on a mission to find - you guessed it - A wetherspoons. I had a quick meal, a couple of pints of Spitfire and back to find 4 policemen hauling Oops further up the beach. Very kind of them, but above high tide is high enough thanks. They seemed concerned about where it had come from and I asked if they had spoken to the Coastguard or the Harbour Master, but they hadn't thought of doing that?? Now I'll have to haul it down tomorrow morning. (I didn't have the heart to ask them to put it back where they found it.) Dover is only 21 miles from France, and 5 months ago I would never have dreamt of crossing the Channel on a Laser, but now it seems like it would be a doddle, 7 miles less than my journey from Ilfracombe to Rhossili Bay. It was on this day in 1831, that Colin Patent Patented the first Patent. He called it a Patent.

CHAPTER 19

DOVER TO SAMPHIRE HOE

<u>Saturday September 11th</u>
I woke before the shipping forecast as usual, and a bit concerned the way the tent was being buffeted in the wind. South west force 4 to 5 increasing to force 6 to 7. Normally I would say, "That's it, let's go back to sleep" but I was so determined to finish this weekend that I decided to try it, albeit reefed right down. Anything other than a south westerly would have given me a chance. I told the coastguard, and asked the Harbour Master if it was safe to go through the harbour entrance, and he confirmed it was OK. I Shot across to the entrance and then met the huge seas just outside. I was tacking as near to the shore as possible to get some protection from Samphire Hoe and eventually Folkestone Harbour, but it was not enough. I managed to get just past Samphire Hoe, and landed on a beach - 5 hours to do about 3 miles. It is a weird place, all the earth dug from the Channel tunnel was dumped here, and a sea wall put round it. The tunnel idea goes back 200 years and in 1880 a 164foot shaft was sunk from the foot of the cliffs, and a tunnel driven 1 1/4 miles out to sea. The place is worth a visit, with some quite rare flowers. Shakespeare Cliff above was where Edgar, a character in King Lear, looks over the brink and cries
"How fearful,
And dizzy 'tis to cast one's eyes so low"
I phoned Hilary to see what the weather reports were like for the next couple of days - SW strong winds, No way was I going to finish soon, so I asked her to come and pick me up, and I will try later next week. What a bummer. (My words - not Edgar's) Hilary arrived and we got a key to get the car almost to the beach, where we got most of my gear, leaving the hull (upside down and at the back of the beach), and spars underneath. I hope it will be safe. When we are born, we are naked, wet, hungry, and we get smacked on the arse. From then on in life gets worse.

<u>Sunday September 12th to Friday September 17th</u>
I spent my time at home listening to the horrendous weather around the country, all coming across the Atlantic as a result of the Hurricane now hitting Jamaica. When I said I was going to the Caribbean with Hilary, someone asked "Jamaica" - I said "No - she wants to go" The same thing happened when we went to Jakarta. (You can vary that old gag, by using Genoa, and Gerona, there must be lots of others - answers on a postcard

please......) Yachts and Yachting did let me have a couple of tickets to the Boat Show so we went and had a good day. We had a sail on a cat, but not as exciting as the Laser - I didn't manage to capsize it once, even though it was quite windy.

CHAPTER 20

SAMPHIRE HOE TO DYMCHURCH

Saturday September 18th
It is still a south westerly 4 to 5 but I decided that as it is forecast to change to the west, it's time to finish off this trip. I packed the bags and off we set for Samphire Hoe. Two hours later and we are on the beach looking at what was left of Oops. They have even pinched the bits that were screwed down this time. All the blocks, Kicker, main-sheet, snap shackles, Map board and compass. There's not a single rope left. Fortunately they couldn't think of what they could use the mast and boom for so they were safe. We drove back home with a list of things that I will have to get. I rummaged through my box of spares and came up with most things, except the main-sheet and Kicking strap. I Whizzed down to Eastbourne to find the chandler's closed (this is 3.30 on a saturday afternoon.) Never mind lets go back to Nick's place - he will lend me the gear from his Laser. I got nearly there when suddenly my rear wheel overtook me. It looks like the bearing retaining nut was not tightened during a service last week, and the wheel literally fell off round a right hander. The good old RAC arrived after an hour, without any means to tow it, having been told that the wheel is not attached, so would need a tow. So let's wait another hour till a tow truck arrives, after going through 2 companies that want their cut. It is getting pricey now - no wonder our RAC membership is so expensive. I eventually got back home at 9.00 without achieving anything today except a massive bill. Still as I always say "null illigitimii carborundum" - (Don't let the bastards grind you down)

Sunday September 19th
With a forecast of west 4 to 5 veering south west and increasing 6, it's still not ideal, but at least the sea looks calmer than of late. Tim gave me a lift to Samphire Hoe, where I phoned the Coastguard, and set off about noon, after putting everything back on Oops. It started and stayed south west all day so I was beating right from the start. I sailed past a red flag (Army) which, fortunately was being taken down, although there had been no mention (again) by the Coastguard that I was going through a firing range, and I eventually got to Dymchurch about 7.00. I dragged Oops up a slipway, next to a Junk. The skipper asked what I had been doing, and said " It must be velly painful sailing around Blitain on a razor". The sea wall here dates back to the Roman times and there are two 19th Century Martello towers, guarding the sluices controlling the water level on Romney Marsh.

Monday September 20th

I don't believe it - the forecast is westerly force 5 to 7 increasing to gale force 8. I phoned the Coastguard who advised against going (what does he know about Laser sailing) Again I was so keen on finishing (only 40 miles left) that I actually got to the waters edge, before putting my sensible head on. A quick phone call to Hilary, can you pick me up and let the Coastguard know I won't be going after all. I had an all day breakfast, then home (again). It took Hilary longer than I expected to get here - I forgot that she had to drive the camper, as our car is still wheel-less. Fortunately Oops is on a slipway so we were able to take the Laser home this time. That way nothing will be stolen. I left London 2 weeks ago and I am still only at Dymchurch. I feel like the frog that jumped from a lily-pad and got half the remaining distance to the riverbank with each jump...... he never did make it ashore.

Tuesday September 21st to Friday September 24th

At home again with Gales everywhere - Ho - Hum. If you can stay calm, while all around you is chaos.... then you probably haven't completely understood the seriousness of the situation. I had a phone call from the mechanic to say the car's fixed so I cycled to Eastbourne to get it. I had a puncture on the way (there's a surprise) I got the car back; along with a zero bill and a bottle of wine from the mechanic - sorry for the inconvenience - (do you think he's trying to tell me it must have been his fault??). I got a phone call in the evening of the 22nd from the Coastguard, asking where I was as they hadn't heard from me. (Hilary forgot to phone them on the 20th).I explained what had happened, and asked them what is their procedure, and they said that my journey was down as an "open issue." and if nobody phones, it remains an open issue????? I'm now not sure why they phoned on the22nd, but I suppose they are actually using some brain power, albeit 2 days after rigor mortis could have set in. Artificial Intelligence is no match for Natural Stupidity.

CHAPTER 21

DYMCHURCH TO EASTBOURNE

Saturday September 25th
North west 3 to 4, veering south west 4 to 5 - That'll do. We packed the car and were back at Dymchurch by 10.30. The Coastguard told me that the firing range is active today, and I will have to go one and a half miles out to sea after Dungeness. I got to Dungeness by 12.00, and spoke to the Safety Boat on the VHF. He knew I was on the way and would escort me round the range. Unfortunately I couldn't fight the current as well as the wind, so after half an hour of going nowhere, I said I would go back to the Lee shore of Dungeness, and beach it for a couple of hours. He escorted me back and stood off for 2 hours, until I was ready to go. Looking back from here there are 2 lighthouses, the new one was built in 1961, because the Nuclear power station blocked the beam of the old lighthouse further inland. - Good planning eh? I set off and got half way past the range with my escort when I was told that they had stopped firing for 2 hours, so I could go where I like.- Great!!. The safety boat left me and I tacked close to shore because here is where the Maanav Star was beached 2 weeks ago. It is a really big ship and looks as though it will be there for some time, although they think they will try to float it off next Monday. Seems pointless until the next spring tides at the end of next week, but why should they ask my opinion. They have been buggering about with diggers and hoses for two weeks without success....I could always give them a tow - Oops can do it!!! I crept past Rye, with the wind easing all the time, and made it to Winchelsea at 6.30, nearly in darkness. The original town was swallowed by the sea during violent storms in the 13th century, but its successor is now nearly 2 miles inland. The retreat of the sea brought about its decline in importance. Winchelsea and Rye were added to the original Cinque Ports in 1336. In the church a window commemorates the 17 man crew of the lifeboat Mary Stanford, lost with all hands in 1928 while trying to reach a ship in distress off Camber Sands. Just after the lifeboat was launched news arrived that the ship's crew had already been rescued. That shoots down Victor Kiam's theory that "Procrastination is opportunity's natural assassin".

Sunday September 26th
It was a north westerly backing westerly force 4, locally 5, according to the shipping forecast. This should be the last day - only 25 miles to go. I started at 7.00 with very little wind, but crept past Fire Hills, so called because in

late spring their slopes are covered with brilliant yellow gorse and into Hastings by 10.30. The sailing club was getting ready for their race, and their rescue boat came out to see what I was doing - I explained and they invited me in for a cup of tea. A great club - the boats are stored in an underground car park right on the beach, and under the road - very secure, I bet they don't get things nicked. I had a quick tea then off along the coast to Bexhill where the sailing club had just finished their races. Pat sails from here, and when I came in to sign their visitor's book, the guns went off, and everyone clapped as I came in the clubhouse (how embarrassing). "Tea or beer?" - "What's the beer?" "Spitfire" "oh go on then, as it's the last day" This is the first time I have indulged whilst still sailing. A quick pint then off at a snails pace to Pevensey Bay S.C. where I signed their book and Photo's were taken. The wind was freshening now (at 3.30) so I shot off to Eastbourne Sovereign S.C. where again the gun salute - Pat had driven from Bexhill to let them know I was on my way. "Tea or beer?" "What beer?" "Harveys" "Oh go on then as it's the last day" Only a quarter of a mile to go to my finish line next to the Pier. I got there with Hilary, Ian, Guy, (and his mum), Pat, Olly and Helen to welcome me in. - thanks guys. Another beer, and back to the Sovereign S.C. where they all helped lift Oops up to the car park. Then guess what - More beers. They had a whip round and presented me with £67 for the Prostate Cancer Charity, in a Lead Crystal Whiskey glass for me with their logo engraved. - A nice touch - what an excuse to take up whiskey drinking. Thanks very much guys.

So I have finished the trip.

This trip has taken 149 days, and I reckon I have covered 3350 miles, but have only sailed on 94 days, that makes an average of 35.6 miles per day, which wasn't far off my original estimate of 30 miles per day. When we cycled round the Coast of Britain in 2002 on our tandem we did 4700 miles in 100 days, which makes 47 miles per day (even I could work that average out).

The campaign began 1st of May,
Round Britain - 30miles a day,
Now that it's done,
I've had so much fun,
P'raps I'll sail round t'other way.

Well that's all folks - if there is anyone who hasn't sponsored me yet, but would like to donate some money, you can always send a cheque to:-
The Prostate Cancer Charity,
3, Angel Walk,
London,
W6 9HX

As I have mentioned, there are still a few challenges left, not necessarily sailing, although I still want to do Ireland, NZ, and Round the IOW race (all on a Laser of course - not necessarily Oops - she may be put out to grass - I have plans for her as a camping dinghy for the Scottish Isles - a dinghy and tent is the way to see them, in my humble opinion). I have asked if Greenwich Council would like to borrow Oops to put next to Gypsy Moth, and the Cutty Sark for a while - I think the contrast would look great. They would have to nail it down though - I can't see it lasting long without some protection,
I quite fancy The Dakar Rally - on a motorbike - none of those wimpy 4 wheeled things, and I think the London Marathon again next year. If anyone can think of any other mad ideas - let me know, and watch this space for future ramblings.

The End

Printed in Great Britain
by Amazon